"If we marvel at a mystic's ability to tread on hot coals or to touch some higher consciousness, we need only realize he is a human using human tools. Whatever he does, we too may do."

Lead yourself into the fascinating world of the soul. If you've seen the incredible feats of the Eastern mystic or felt the awesome power of psychic events, you have glimpsed the power of the Soul. MAN'S UNENDING QUEST will teach you of the Soul:

- You will learn what the Soul is, how it works and why it uses human flesh.

- You will learn that ancient wisdom sleeps within it, waiting for you to release it.

- You will learn how it can lead you to a more satisfying and fulfilling life.

- And you will learn that you are never alone, for your Soul has loving Guides who will someday share your Destiny.

Here, in these pages, Man's quest bears fruit. With the patient guidance of Higher Souls, Robert Allan Stewart carefully explains the essence of the human Soul.

YOU WILL NEVER READ A BOOK SO MUCH A PART OF YOUR LIFE

MAN'S UNENDING QUEST

by

Robert Allan Stewart

1984
LLEWELLYN PUBLICATIONS
St. Paul, Minnesota, 55164-0383, U.S.A.

Copyright © 1984
by Robert Allan Stewart

All rights reserved. No part of this book, either in part or in whole, may be reproduced, transmitted or utilized in any form or by any means electronic, photographic or mechanical, including photocopying, recording, or by any information storage or retrieval system, without permission in writing from the Publisher, except for brief quotations embodied in literary articles and reviews.

For permission, or for serialization, condensation, or for adaptation, write to the publisher at the address below.

International Standard Book Number: 0-87542-750-2
Library of Congress Catalog Card Number: 84-21875

First Edition, 1984
First Printing, 1984

Library of Congress Cataloging in Publication Data
Stewart, Robert Allan, 1956-
  Man's unending quest.

  Bibliography: p.
  1. Spirit writings   I. Title.
BF1301.S74   1984   133.9'3   84-21875
ISBN 0-87542-750-2 (pbk.)

Cover Art: Philip M. Jacobson

Published by
LLEWELLYN PUBLICATIONS
A Division of Chester-Kent, Inc.
P.O. Box 64383
St. Paul, MN 55164-0383, U.S.A.

Printed in the United States of America

To My Wife

Table of Contents

Foreword		ix
Introduction		xiii
Chapter 1:	The Soul	1
Chapter 2:	Humanity's Purpose	27
Chapter 3:	Man's Imperfect Truth	51
Chapter 4:	The Whole Truth vs. Partial Truth	79
Chapter 5:	The Creator	107
Chapter 6:	The Crossroads of Man	129
Chapter 7:	The Cultivation of Man	153
Chapter 8:	The Mystique of Mysticism	177
Chapter 9:	The Science of Metaphysics	197
Appendix		209
Glossary		215
Bibliography		223

THE LIFE-CYCLE OF THE SOUL

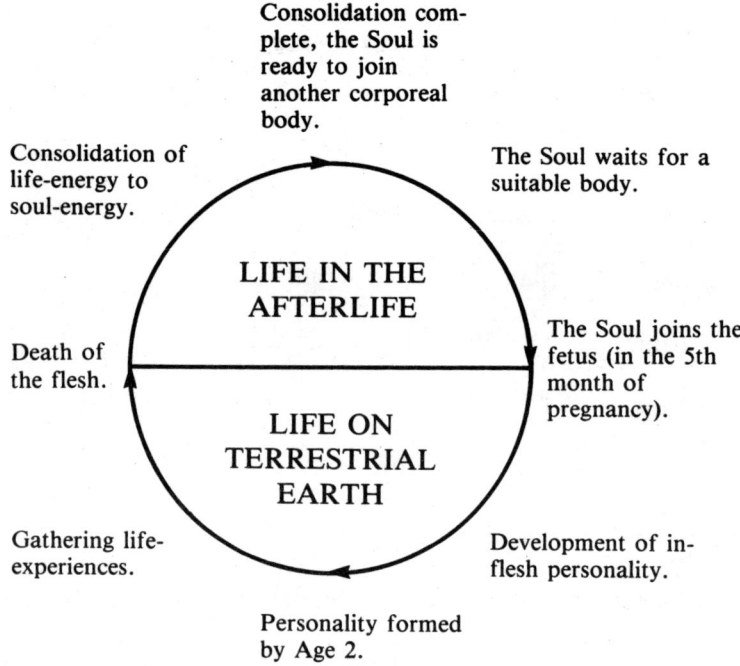

Figure 1.

FOREWORD

Man's purpose is to evolve, just as every living being must evolve. Man is only one of the many divisions of evolution; his is not a great division but merely the division between those above and those below. Thus, he is not to revere himself above all other lifeforms as he is so wont to do, especially if they happen to be lesser than he. There are many lifeforms greater than man; many facets of his own existence he refuses to understand because they are not readily perceived by his five basic senses. Man can train himself to perceive and understand these unknowns only if he overcomes his doubt and fear. This is no easy task: his own mythologies, superstitions and fairytales describe many frightening and horrible things that inspire more fear and doubt than understanding. All humans, no matter what their culture or customs, have remarkably similar impressions of life beyond their known world.

Consider the prevalence of witches, fairies, goblins, devils, ghosts, spirits and a host of other mysterious entities which pervade his folklore and religions. Modern man is inclined to debunk these spiritual manifestations as no more than the workings of imagination. Doubters often forget that all fantasy has some foundation in fact. Much of the doubt focuses on the name and supposed characteristics of these unknown entities. Witches and magic are debunked

Man's Unending Quest

as myth and trickery, yet mediums and magicians work wonders that make untutored minds marvel. That witches are called mediums in Western societies means only that the word medium is more acceptable; it does not deny that certain persons, primarily women, have inordinate abilities scarcely understood by man. That magicians are known to use physical laws to their advantage does not subtract from the wonder of their feats. Man's mind is clogged by his own doubts and constipated by his fears of the unknown. He casts around himself a veil of ignorance that is compounded by the limitations of his senses.

There are lifeforms beyond man's known world. That is fact and it is also fact that these lifeforms are from time to time manifested in some ways in this world. Their names and characteristics could well be the workings of man's imagination but the reality of their existence is not. The existence of these unexplained and often unperceived entities, like his own existence, is part of the interrelation of a universe that extends in far more complex directions than the space and time he knows. The universe is more than that which is perceived by man's senses and machinery; man has hardly begun to explore the infinite complexity of worlds within the range of his perceptions. Telescopes may bring distant stars into clearer focus but many other worlds are near at hand. Only man himself can now explore them, for they are beyond the range of any machine he has yet devised. But to reach those worlds, he must first reach beyond his sensory perceptions, deeper into his own self and put aside his superstitious fears of the unknown. He must call upon talents he rarely realizes he possesses and use them wisely. Above all, he must recognize the existence of his soul and how it may help him.

As an individual, you must learn to balance the levels of your being to allow your mind to pierce the veil of ignorance. You must recognize that the knowledge of your

Foreword

soul will never harm you if you do not allow your fear and imagination to rule your mind. You must free yourself of your fear of death, for the soul never dies. It grows only greater with the gathered wisdom of all your lives in flesh. And you must heed the laws of Karma, which balance the forces of this planet. Do not let the concepts of Karma and Reincarnation deter you from seeking your truth, for you can know in your mind the same truths known to your soul — that your soul will survive the death of this corporeal body and will someday join another. Let your wisdom be your guide; and balance the harm you do in this world with many acts of good. Your truth is locked in the soul that is your life. You must only reach that truth to be free of doubt. Then how you use this knowledge is up to you.

Author's Note: These words were given to me as my introduction to this work. They were dictated to me through a mystic channel by entities I can only describe as higher beings who share our planet. These unseen guides are a part of our lives in many ways we don't fully understand; they have often been described in our religions and myths as gods and they have much to teach us. In the following book, I endeavor to accurately pass on what they have taught me. Even though we don't understand who or what these guides are, their quest, like ours, is tied to this fragile planet. Perhaps that is why they teach us.

R.A.S.

INTRODUCTION

Man is engaged in a quest. His quest is essentially the same as that of every other animal on this planet: the quest for survival. Yet man has added to this basic quest like no other animal. He has evolved higher motivations and has set for himself greater tasks. In so doing, he has achieved the only true measure of difference between himself and the so-called lower orders: civilization.

Man's civilization, though ultimately the result of his basic quest to survive, is such an intricate network of social and architectural constructs that he has convinced himself he is somehow more than a mere animal. Yet try as he might, he has not been able to define what sets him apart from his lesser brothers. He has explored his physiology and has found that apart from his opposable thumb and relatively large brain he has little to set him apart biologically. Even at that, there are other species that possess these qualities, though they use them with less skill. To prove his higher nature, man has at various times claimed that he is the only animal to reason, use tools, learn language and create art. Yet one by one, these notions have been proven false. Many animals use crude tools in their natural environment, the chimpanzee even fashioning simple tools to aid in gathering food. This same animal also reasons extremely well. Human teachers have taught chimpanzees sign language and to paint pictures mistaken for works of the avant garde. Man has found, often to his chagrin, that he is not as unique as he thought.

Though not so different biologically, some have claimed man is the only animal to possess a soul. This argument, like the others, stems more from the desire of some humans to set themselves above and apart from other animals than any fundamental difference in nature. It is, however, the last argument of this sort to be proved wrong. No one has ever empirically proved the existence of the soul. Although this book does not prove the soul exists, it argues emphatically that man does have a soul, that this soul survives bodily death and that its existence can and will be empirically proved. This soul is based in physical life-energy similar to that of other animals. Man's soul differs from the souls of other highly evolved mammals only to the same degree that their biological (or corporeal) bodies differ. What man continually finds is that it is not his nature that is different, but his context. And he has made this context himself.

Man's greater intellect has enabled him to dominate his world. Perhaps it is his ongoing rape of this world that compels him to claim divine right, though he acts on his own lusts. As he builds his civilizations, he tears down much of his natural world. Though he often seeks justification, he has none but his ability and power to do as he pleases. Yet there is much that is good about man's quest. He has elevated his simple struggle to survive to a complex quest for knowledge. This need to know is almost as great as his need to survive. For ages, men have risked death (some, like Socrates, have openly accepted death) in pursuit of knowledge. This quest has driven them to the depths of the atom and to the far reaches of space. If man's primary need is to survive, then knowledge is certainly his secondary need.

This need to know is more than just a desire to improve

Introduction

his physical condition. Man has an innate desire to know that presses him to endure great hardship in his chosen tasks. Such motivation *must* derive from a source other than the corporeal body and that source is the soul.

The soul is a real, physical part of the human being, based in energy forms man has yet to analyze and understand. Yet man does recognize the soul; every known human society has developed beliefs and traditions regarding the soul's survival of bodily death. Although this evidence is circumstantial at best, it is more than exists for the opposing view. Those individuals who say there is no soul have not even a tradition to follow. Because I longed to know the truth, I engaged in a quest of my own. By exploring techniques long used by occultists and mystics, I was able to explore some of the principles of the soul. I know now that the soul does survive the death of the flesh. I only lack the empirical evidence that would convince the impartial skeptic. Thus, much of the information I present in these pages must be offered on the basis of personal testimony, even though I am personally confident in its accuracy. When my contemporaries relegate such concepts as life-after-death, reincarnation and the soul to the obscure regions of the supernatural, I fear they forget that lightning bolts were also once regarded as supernatural.

The skeptic must always be prepared to be surprised. Many scientists, though not wanting to touch anything tainted by the word soul, nonetheless long to know the source of human life. In effort to learn this secret, scientists have tried to construct a discipline that studies the soul without directly admitting they are doing so. Thus, they created psychology, now considered the study of the human mind (a more palatable term for many scientists). The name itself, however, is derived from the Greek word *psyche*, which means soul. Likewise, parapsychology evolved because psychology has failed to reach deeply enough into the human consciousness to explain everything that consciousness does. Although often derided as thoroughly as psychology was in *its* infancy, parapsychology has since the 1930s demonstrated the existence of nonsensory events such as extrasensory perception (ESP) and psychokinesis (PK). These nonsensory events of human consciousness are products of the soul. They go unexplained because so far, science refuses to look for a physical cause of consciousness beyond the corporeal body. Both psychology and parapsychology were created as disciplines because of the need to explore human consciousness. Both disciplines have so far failed to explain all the events of consciousness, both sensory and nonsensory. They have failed to define the soul.

This book is the result of my efforts to force a new direction in the study of the human soul. I have tried to construct a coherent theory which binds together what is already known of the soul and what I have learned through mystic techniques. This, then, is a consolidation of knowledge. Because of the religious associations with the word soul, I must stress that I have no religious affiliations. I have tried throughout my research to let science be my guide in making rational assimilations of facts.

At this point, I must also stress that my methods of gathering facts have necessarily differed from the controlled laboratory experiments preferred by modern science. I have indeed delved into the occult, an area that should instead be called metaphysics. In doing so, I have learned a great deal about the hidden side of man. I have also learned a great deal about the hidden side of myself, have witnessed my own greatest weaknesses and failings and have had to face them. I acknowledge this now because it was facing up to my inner self which enabled me to break through to the lower levels of my consciousness and to be accepted by guides who do not fit into modern science's scheme of things at all. In other words, when the facts known to science failed

Introduction

me, I went looking on my own and found more than I ever dreamed possible. As a result, I have been forced to discard many of my beliefs, beliefs that were carefully instilled by social training in an emerging secular Western society with a Christian history. In their place, I have what I consider to be a truer picture of human life and evolution.

There are many areas of historical tradition that, although ostensibly mythology, religion or folklore, do contain very real elements of truth. Reincarnation, a concept my Western upbringing inspired me to loathe, was eventually proved to me to be real; my reading of man's religious mythology also indicated that two-thirds of the human population hold it as a serious belief.* Belief in life-after-death is even more widespread. Science is only now seriously considering the possibility that the human personality can survive the death of the body. Other areas are also gradually coming under the suspicious gaze of scientists. Faith healing, revelation and the "religious experience" are attracting some attention; magic, sorcery and witchcraft, the dark sisters of human fear, provide further fertile ground for research into the effects of ritual. The human world is steeped in mysticism and spirituality; the universality of many beliefs and the similarity of ritualistic practices point to governing laws of behavior. In these areas, therefore, lie clues to the human soul. Further clues lie in individual experiences that go beyond the usual.

Over the years, I have experienced many paranormal events. Even so, I was long unable to accept many concepts of mysticism because I had no direct experience of those particular concepts. I, like most people, relied on my personal perceptions to guide me in the acceptance of fact

---

*More, if you count the Christian belief in selective reincarnation. The founding principle of Christianity is the return of Christ, the Second Coming, which can be interpreted as being the reincarnation of Christ. Further, there is the belief, written in Matthew 11.14, that John the Baptist was the reincarnated prophet Elijah.

and, when perceptions were not available, I relied on conventional wisdom. When I learned certain occult techniques, however, I launched myself into a new appreciation for the unknown. Instead of randomly encountering unexplainable events, such as precognition, I suddenly became able to deliberately engage in psychic phenomena. The technique I found most successful and which provided me with the basis of this book was automatic writing. This technique is easy to describe but for most people difficult to achieve. You simply set a pen to paper and allow a consciousness other than your own mind to guide it. I found that my own deeper consciousness, my soul, could guide the pen and that other souls could guide it. Without ever being a natural medium, I learned to be a medium. My greatest advantage, I soon realized, was that I didn't lose consciousness as many natural psychics do when acting as a medium. I was therefore totally aware of what was occurring, transcribing the thoughts of another mind (or soul) as they were communicated to me. When automatic writing, of course, I had no idea of what was being communicated until I received the communication. The sentences unravelled behind my pen while my consciousness stood passively by.

There are many people who have experienced automatic writing; probably many more who have tried and failed. What I know of the technique, I have described in the Appendix. There are also many books describing the technique, including transcriptions, some of which I have listed in the annotated bibliography. Comparing Arthur Conan Doyle's (creator of Sherlock Holmes) book *Pheneas Speaks* with those written by Eileen Sullivan and Ruth Montgomery will quickly provide an idea of what is possible through automatic writing. Whether through chance or design, I have been able to structure my book according to my own thoughts, guided by the souls who have communi-

Introduction

cated with me over the years. Thus, this book is not about automatic writing or mediumship, but about the soul. I have attempted to construct a clear and comprehensive theory, albeit vastly simplified, of what the soul is, how it functions and how it fits into the human experience. Although nothing can convince the devout skeptic but personal experience, I hope the theory I present will sound reasonable enough to even those who have had no paranormal experiences. For those who have studied the existing literature of metaphysics and psychical research, this book should ring true.

As for the guides who assisted me so greatly in this writing, I know that some of them are human souls of the Afterlife and that others, the primary agents of my instruction, are not. These others have never fully described themselves to me yet they have told me that they have never lived on this plane in human flesh. Their world is another plane than this one, another plane than the Afterlife. Their plane, and many others, coexists with ours in the same finite space. The physical nature of these planes are such that they exist on a continuum, just as radio frequencies exist on a spectrum. These other planes, including the Afterlife, consist of matter far less dense than atomical matter and are on occasion perceived by in-flesh humans because of the non-atomical part of the human being, the soul. These occasions lead us to create our myths of other worlds and of gods, demons, spirits and ghosts. Although our myths do not accurately reflect reality, they are stimulated by reality. It is up to us to determine in what ways they are real.

As my work on this book progressed, I found much of the information presented to me by my guides to be independently verifiable. I was not trying to find the lost city of Atlantis, query the existence of God or create a new philosophical tradition. I only wanted to find out if there was life after this and to my satisfaction, I found the answer. Furthermore, I found much that I was not overtly seeking.

Man's Unending Quest

Whenever possible, I researched the information given to me during a period of instruction. To my surprise, I readily found documentary sources in museums, libraries and bookstores that corroborated what I just learned. To my even greater surprise, I often walked into a bookstore or library and went directly to the shelf and book that provided information in an area I was studying. Just as often, I would open a book to precisely the right passage. It didn't seem to matter if the book was new or used, whether I had read it or if I even knew what was in it. The dictionary became a magic tool, opening to let my eyes fall on a word fitting the meaning I was groping for. Always, the information I was guided to supported what my guides were teaching me. It was as if they wanted to show me what man already knew and despite my doubts, there was documentation to be had.

My guides have always encouraged me to read. Although reading does not convince the reader of anything he is not prepared to accept, it often helps ideas to congeal and provides a broader base of knowledge on which to form opinions. The major test of my work is its ability to help others in their rationalization of human life. No matter what you choose to believe, there is absolutely no harm in entertaining new ideas. Knowledge does not harm you. It is how you use it that is important. Thus, I present some information in this book which has no documentation to support it other than the bald statement as fact or theory. Still, the information is important and should be available for those who want to think about it. A case in point is the statement in Chapter 1 that driving the soul out of the body at death consumes the energy equivalent of operating a one-watt light bulb for one-third of one second. Man at this point has no machine that can measure soul-energy. Yet I leave the statement exactly as I received it. I am confident that it will one day be proved correct.

In writing this book, I have found many other books

Introduction

to be profoundly useful, some because of the information they contain, others because of how they reveal human nature. Thus, I have compiled a small bibliography which I hope will steer the interested to related works. The list is primarily intended as a means of casting a wider loop than a single book can. I also hope that the books add weight to what I say, especially concerning facets of reality not readily acknowledged by conventional Western thought. ESP, for example, I consider a proved fact of human existence, based on the extensive statistical evidence gathered by such researchers as Joseph and Louisa Rhine of Duke University. This evidence has been tested and retested, the experiments replicated again and again. It is now certain that some people have more than the normal amount of extrasensory ability (or *psi*, as parapsychologists have dubbed it), while all of us seemingly possess some. From my personal experience, I know what they have found is indeed true. If people still doubt the facts, I can only offer references to the literature. Thus, I hope to offer the means to pursue my ideas and statements to their logical conclusion.

I also find that many people doubt what I consider indisputable, that is, elements of my experience. I was first drawn to study parapsychology because of precognitive episodes I first experienced in my preteens. From time to time, I dream of something that seems to have no special relevance until some time later when this dream starts occurring all over again — but in real life. In other words, I occasionally see an instant out of my future as clearly in the dream as when the event actually happens. I don't know why this happens or when it will happen again. There seems to be no special meaning to any of the events, though they often concern something, someplace or somebody entirely new to me. Once, on a trail ride, I suddenly realized I had experienced a moment of it before. The riders and their mounts, the surroundings and even my emotions were exactly as they were in a dream a few weeks before. I lived that brief portion of my life twice, as I have lived many other moments twice. The most stunning case of precognition I have had was during a period of intense instruction by my guides when I asked to be shown in a dream what would occur the next day. As I slept, I glimpsed scenes that although as strange as any fantasy dream, turned out exactly so the next day. In fact, the events were so peculiar, involving occult techniques I had never known before, that I could not possibly have engineered them in any form of "self-fulfilled destiny".

In spite of the indubitable nature of the experience, I often meet people who say it is impossible to foresee the future. They insist that it is impossible because science has not yet found how it can be possible. However, when precognition is experienced as plainly as any other experience, it becomes plain that science has more research to do. I don't know yet how precognition works but I believe my prescient dreams are a result of points of "stasis" in my life, points at which major elements of my consciousness are in a particular harmony. I explore the concept of stasis further in the text but for now it illustrates this point. I believe that my experiences of precognition relate not so much to the events themselves as qualities of the soul which enable them to happen. The soul, then, is aware of what will happen before it actually does. This knowledge, usually hidden from the waking mind, can be brought to the mind's attention by a mechanism of consciousness not often used. Discovering what this mechanism is and how it works, therefore, could lead us to have far greater control over our lives.

Studying the soul is not a fanciful occupation. It is a study of your own life and has very real consequences for you and for humanity. I have attempted in this book to consolidate much of what is known about the soul with what

Introduction

I have learned from my guides. Thus, many of the ideas herein should be familiar to those who have studied metaphysics. I have attempted to filter my guides' teachings through a skeptical mind, in view of writing for other skeptical minds. I have attempted whenever and however possible to verify these teachings and to pass them on as true to their original form as I can. I hope others will be stimulated by this work to renew man's interest in the soul. The soul as much as any other part of reality is there to be explored; it need not remain in the cloudy realm of faith. Perhaps some readers will be encouraged to attempt automatic writing. If so, the cautionary words of the Appendix should be well heeded. In this and any other work in the occult, use wisdom as your closest guide.

1

THE SOUL

There is a soul in the human body, as there is in all living beings. That this soul is real, a part of you, does not mean it is all of you or even the ascendent part of you. You also have a mind and a body and together they provide the experience of the human being.

The soul is a physical part of the universe and is dependent on all the forces and natural laws that direct the universe. There is nothing about it that is "supernatural" or beyond physical reality. It is simply undefined. We tend, as human beings, to define our universe according to our five primary senses. Most of all, we depend on sight. That we depend so much on a single ability means only that we restrict our other abilities — a dog, for instance, relies more on his sense of smell. Yet because of the limitations of our primary senses, many of us refuse to believe we each have a soul. We cannot see it, therefore we believe it isn't there. But the soul should not be so easily denied. It is real. You cannot taste, smell or hear your soul, nor can you truly touch it. It can be "felt" in certain oblique ways but not in the normal manner of gathering sensory experience. And only under certain conditions can you actually see a manifestation of soul, though not the soul itself. That is because the human senses function on atomically related principles while the soul does not. Yet this is no reason to doubt the soul's existence. Men once for the same reason refused to believe air existed.

Unlike air, which is for the most part a random collection of gases, there is very little random about the soul. It is not gaseous nor even atomical. Instead, it consists of two highly organized energy types, both closely related in form and structure but differing enormously in certain properties. The primary energy is called "soul-energy"* and forms the core of your being. It is the physical base for consciousness and as such is called, simply, the base soul. It is the ultimate root of intelligence, although the energy matter itself is not intelligent in the rational sense. It holds only life; the awareness associated with this life is called the base conscious. The secondary energy is called "life-energy". Life-energy forms the base for an upper conscious, or mind. It is actually a different energy structure than the base soul, and is incorporated into the base soul after the death of the flesh. The life-energy structure is produced by the base soul functioning in a corporeal body — the body, by converting food energy to life-energy, sustains the life-energy structure.

The life-energy structure is called the "Spirit". It is superimposed on the base soul as virtually an independent consciousness. It is formed during an incarnation in flesh (or a human lifetime, to phrase it differently) and is

---

*There is natural etymology in communications involving the soul that has been deliberately evolved by souls and passed on to me (in part at least) by my guides. They have been very explicit in how terms and usages of selected "soul-words" are to appear in this work. When using a language such as English (souls also can communicate with each other in a direct ESP-like communication), souls must discern appropriate usages. If terms are not strictly applied, more so than in this world, ambiguity results. This, I presume, is because of the circumstances of life in the Afterlife. The souls also use their preferred etymology in communication with in-flesh humans. For example, it has been made very clear to me that to "gather" experience is a correct usage whereas to "accumulate" experience is not. Gather, therefore, is a soul-word. The terminology developed in this work is perhaps not entirely the work of my guides, as I have been obliged to construct terms myself. I believe, however, that all usages are correct and acceptable and I have defined them as much as possible in the glossary at the end of this book.

The Soul

essentially the personality you are familiar with as being *you*. Underlying this level of consciousness is the base soul, which is the physical manifestation of all the experiences of all your previous incarnations in flesh. Thus, life-energy exists to capture the experiences of the life you are now living. When your body dies, your base soul and Spirit will return to the Afterlife where these new experiences will be consolidated with all previous experiences. In the process, some of the life-energy will be lost as simple heat and all that remains of the Spirit will be converted to soul-energy. The base soul that then emerges will be free to join another body to create a new Spirit and gather more life-experience.

The corporeal body only survives when it is physically joined with a base soul. When the base soul leaves the flesh, the flesh dies. While in flesh, the soul does not leave, even for an instant. Life-energy, on the other hand, as encapsulated in the Spirit, can and does leave the flesh for brief periods. This phenomena is known as astral projection, or Spirit Travel, which some in-flesh humans have mistakenly described as the soul leaving the body. In actual fact, the base soul remains behind during such excursions and maintains the biological functions of the organism. When the travelling Spirit returns, normal sleeping or waking consciousness returns to the organism. The human mind, as the prime element of awareness of the Spirit, remembers these projections in terms it is familiar with, or submerges them to the unconscious.

Both the base soul and the Spirit (Soul, with a capital,*

---

*When translating the thoughts of a soul to a written language, certain constraints result. Souls, therefore, encourage the use of capitals to denote subtle distinctions of meaning between terms. Thus, Soul refers to the entire life structure, base soul and Spirit combined. In this sense, Spirit itself denotes a specific meaning beyond the generalized usage of the word "spirit", as in the usage "of good spirits". The capitalization denotes a specific definable entity. Thus, the Spirit is one definable unit of life which is a subpart of a larger definable unit called the Soul. Another usage that will be reflected in my work is the definition of the term Earth. Because the English language uses "earth" to refer to this ball of atomical matter on which

Man's Unending Quest

is the base soul and the Spirit considered together as a single unit, usually after the death of the flesh; see Figure 1 at the front of the book for a schematic of the life-cycle) consist of energy particles tinier than the principle constituents of the atom. While in flesh, both the base soul and the Spirit have form and definition related to that corporeal structure. The two "astral bodies", as they are sometimes called, pervade the atomical matter of the corporeal body, much like liquid holding solids in suspension. The particles of soul- and life-energy may move freely through the particles of the atoms but are essentially confined to the same area. (Psychic students are aware of the aura, the visible manifestation of life-energy which surrounds the body. The aura is a manifestation of the Spirit which pervades the entire body and extends outwards, creating a visible aura around its outer edge.) Because of the relationship with the body, the base soul and Spirit take shape and form from that body. When out of flesh, the Soul does not need to adhere to the human shape but does need some definition of form. Thus, it usually retains its human "shape" because of its familiarity with the form.

The life-energy of the Spirit is far less stable than the soul-energy. Soul-energy, once formed, has a relatively permanent existence — "relatively permanent" because it is organized in such a way that it will survive longer than the material earth we cherish. This longevity is only possible because of the cyclical process of reincarnation which ensures that the soul-energy will never be destabilized by lack of reconstitution. As any complex energy structure is prone to breaking down into simpler energy forms (in physics, this is known as the Second Law of Thermodynamics), the Soul must consistently replenish itself with new energy. This

---

we live, souls use the lower case term to refer to the atomical portion of the planet ("terrestrial" earth). However, there are many more levels of matter beyond the atomical and when considered in the aggregate, they constitute the planet Earth.

The Soul

process occurs through reincarnation, the incarnations of the flesh providing the necessary raw material. In the case of humanity, the corporeal body produces the life-energy primarily from the food consumed. Thus, the body is a mechanism for converting food-energy into life-energy, a process directed by various levels of consciousness.

While in flesh, the human being requires a vast amount of energy. For the most part, this energy can be witnessed in its devolving form, body heat. The life-energy structure, the Spirit, is so unstable that it constantly breaks down into simpler energy forms, including heat and, in specific circumstances, electrically related energies. As the human being goes about his daily life, his body functions to maintain both the corporeal structure, also in need of constant replenishment, and the life-energy structure. When life-energy breaks down, like the corporeal body, the natural reconstitution process enables the reconstruction of exactly the same form. In other words, the Spirit does not change in form very much over time, though the actual particles of energy are exchanged constantly. When the incarnation is complete, the life-energy structure is removed from the flesh with the base soul. While the base soul and Spirit are united with the flesh, the flesh survives. If the base soul separates from the flesh, the flesh dies and begins to decompose. The soul, in effect, is the glue that holds the body together.

Because the corporeal body has certain cohesive properties which bind the soul to it, a minute amount of energy is consumed by the separation process at death. This energy is taken from the life-energy of the mind, though the mind itself (as a human consciousness) may be unaware of the exchange. The life-energy therefore drives the soul from the flesh, taking itself with it. Through this process, the mind and supporting Spirit survive as a unified awareness, though the nature of awareness differs greatly when removed from flesh. The minute bit of mind-energy consumed by the separation process is dissipated as simple heat and amounts to the electrical equivalent of operating a one-watt light bulb for one-third of one second.

At the point of death, the reaction between mind (and its supporting Spirit) and base soul is one of merging, much like the soluble action of sugar in water. Two distinct forms of energy matter, similar in structure but differing in specific properties, are brought together as an aware and functional unit, the Soul. The base soul now has ascendency over the mind, the opposite effect to what happens during waking consciousness when in flesh. Even so, the mind remains an active and organized force. Because its circumstances are remarkably altered, it must react to the new situation both in terms of rational intelligence and according to the physical laws acting upon it. For some humans, the rejoining of the Afterlife is a traumatic experience. For others, it is exceptionally pleasant. The necessary fact to realize here is that there is no Heaven or Hell, no place of punishment or degradation. There is just the wholesome renewal of a different phase of life.

The Afterlife is a place common to all human souls and to many of our animal brethren. Each form of life has its own properties of energy renewal but all basically require the same cyclical approach. There is a pattern to the universe that is essentially cyclical in nature, involving the building up and breaking down of matter, and we humans are a part of the process. We see during in-flesh life the results of age and debility. We do not, however, see the rejuvenation that occurs after the death of the flesh. The experiences gathered in that incarnation survive with the soul and are taken into the Afterlife to be studied and made a part of the soul's vast collage of experience. The soul holds the experiences of all its lives locked deep in memories which in-flesh humans sometimes call upon. These experiences are sometimes

The Soul

frightening or disorienting, often occurring during sleep as dreams, but are essentially a natural force of life. Our daily experiences, far from being random events, are planned moments that necessitate certain reactions and actions on our part. We must foment an attitude of learning throughout our lives to enrich these experiences. Even death itself is a planned moment: the soul joins the flesh at a planned moment and leaves it at a planned moment. There is no random chance; only selective choice and the necessary repercussions of those choices.

Because the soul is life, it must renew itself over time. As a lifeform, too, it must constantly improve itself and its ability to survive. If it didn't, it would debilitate in much the same manner as the corporeal body ages. Through the continuing process of reincarnation, the soul constantly improves itself and evolves into greater and greater truths. Its evolution may be fast or slow relative to others around it or it may seem to lie dormant for long periods. Whatever the personal choices of the soul (for the soul does choose its own Way) the process of reincarnation must in one way or another be used.

In the process of reincarnation, the corporeal body is used to generate life-energy and provide experiences of life. As the soul learns greater and greater truths, it learns to improve and modify its behavior so that its existence improves. Its motivation is the same as that of the in-flesh human being: pleasure, comfort and security of survival. As it adds to itself over time, both through experience and the quantitative addition of energy, the soul becomes a greater entity. At certain points, it changes its character drastically, perhaps joining a new physical plane (atomical earth is only one of our planet's many planes*) or a new

---
*One point my guides have so far left me to work out for myself is the actual number of planes, including the atomical earth and the Human Afterlife, there are in the planet Earth. My subjective impression is 21, plus smaller semi-

species. Humans are only a part of a chain of progression, beginning at a point far into the past and extending far into the future. Each human soul will eventually stop reincarnating on earth in human flesh and will join a higher world and a higher form of astral flesh. In the meantime, we all continue to reincarnate on earth, doing the things humans like to do. We add to our experience and to our souls, using our bodies as vehicles for evolution.

For life-experiences to be incorporated into the basic soul structure, a period of consolidation must occur in the Afterlife. When the base soul and Spirit merge together in the Afterlife, the process of consolidation begins. There are two faces to this consolidation, one being the physical incorporation of the life-energy structure into the base soul and the second the resolution of the life-experiences of the immediate incarnation with those of prior incarnations. This consolidation period follows every incarnation and, like minor steps along the way, certain other forms of consolidation occur while the soul remains in flesh. Although the incorporation of life-energy into the primary soul-structure adds to the soul's physical base, the quantitative addition is slight. The gradual addition of matter over many incarnations is like the rings added to a tree with each year's growth. Although the soul's dependencies are far different than the tree's, the process of life is basically the same.

Although the soul can exist indefinitely as a unified entity, it cannot exist indefinitely without change and reorganization. The experiences of each incarnation are

---

independent regions of physical reality known as "bridges", which sometimes bridge two planes. On each plane, there is room for life to grow and evolve. If no other truth is accepted by the reader of this book, this one fact should be: these other planes are not only your past but your future and when one, such as atomical earth, is tampered with, all others are affected. The human experiment on earth carries much damage to other worlds as well. Yet we still cannot control our own expansive urges to shape a world's destiny.

The Soul

carried with the energy matter that make up the soul to the next life. Each salvaged experience is oriented as part of the actual soul-structure, the arrangement of energy particles which constitute the soul. The experiences retained in this manner may be re-envisioned and "experienced" again much as you can remember a passage or event from yesterday or your childhood. The recollection is absolute — it is as precise as your perception at the time allowed. In this sense, the soul remembers much like the iron oxide on magnetic tape "remembers" a song or videotape "remembers" visual impressions.

With the transformation of life-energy into the more stable soul-energy, there is an inevitable loss of energy, and hence experience, as waste heat. The life-energy is not fully converted to soul-energy as nature commands all forces of energy to create byproducts. Thus, the experiences of an incarnation are one by one measured for their usefulness and significance and melded with the experiences of other lives. Some of these lives may have contributed much to the overall experience of the soul, having been incarnations geared towards a consolidation of experience. Others may seem simply to be a gathering of life-experience, just the usual events of living in flesh. As the experiences are resolved with the past-life experiences (those of prior incarnations), the conscious awareness of the soul sees how it has improved its past behavior and how its improvements may be improved further through the next incarnation. It is at this point that a direction or course of evolution begins to form. The soul, having learned much already, must base its further evolution on that base of experience and plan its next life. Once in flesh, the submerged base soul will again provide the pivotal direction that a new mind and Spirit will use to choose its actions in life.

When the consolidation process is complete, the soul is prepared to join another corporeal body. All the experiences of the immediately prior incarnation have been consolidated with those of the past lives. Experiences lost during consolidation (very few are) with rare exception are only the routine and mundane matters of maintaining the flesh. In any incarnation, things such as avoiding mud puddles and talking about the weather provide a wide collage of experience but are in total of little significance. Many of the more significant events of an incarnation happen in a few moments, not the least of which is the death of the flesh. That moment, perhaps, has more significance than any other.

When the last experiences of the incarnation have been consolidated, the life-energy structure, the Spirit, has effectively ceased to exist. The soul is at that point more unified than it is at any other and is prepared to embark on a new adventure in the flesh. The joining may not occur for some time after consolidation and the soul may wish in the meantime to retain in ascendency many of the characteristics of its most recent life (after all, the most recent life is the most evolved so far). It therefore has most of the qualities associated with the immediately prior incarnation, such as personality traits and even general appearance, though they are altered by the more intense physical reality of the Afterlife. Once the soul has achieved consolidation, that process cannot be reversed. When it joins the flesh again, it does so as a greater soul than it was before its prior evolution. It may make mistakes, but will never regress in time or evolution. (The Hindu philosophy, therefore, that errors made on earth cause regression of the soul to lower lifeforms is not correct. Errors in judgement may hinder a soul's evolution but will not subtract from the soul's current physical status. In fact, during consolidation in the Afterlife, the soul will recognize its mistakes and, ideally, try to correct them in coming incarnations.)

In joining a body, the soul is then physically prepared

The Soul

to begin the construction of a new mind and new Spirit. This new Spirit will be the primary influence of that incarnation, the result of the processes that meld the experience of the soul with the new corporeal body. As geneticists have established, the corporeal body itself has a memory of past evolution. It shows evidence of this memory in its embryonic development, exhibiting the various stages of biological evolution before the fetus takes human form. The single-celled ovum and sperm join to form an entity that grows through cell-splitting to become a multi-celled organism. It then evolves fish-like, amphibian, reptilian and finally mammalian characteristics before becoming decidedly human. Also the biological characteristics of species are guaranteed (barring mutations) as long as normal biological processes are not interrupted. Furthermore, specific familial characteristics are passed on from parents to child, such as size, facial features and hair color.

The genetic structure of the organism can be "read" by the soul, which can trace the biological evolution of the corporeal body through association with that body. These genetic memories are not so obvious to the mind, though the mind can sometimes tap the soul's awareness of the body's biological history. The soul usually gains an inherent knowledge of this biological history the moment it joins the flesh in the womb through the natural reactions of two dissimilar but reactive physical substances coming into direct contact. Even before joining the flesh, however, the soul can assimilate enough information about a body's characteristics to know whether it is suitable for its projected tasks for that incarnation. When the soul joins the flesh (usually in the fifth month of pregnancy, for that is when the fetus can potentially survive outside the womb if aborted) it brings with it soul-memories of many past lives and the bodies used in those lives. These characteristics are blended with those of the new body and a new personality begins to form.

Man's Unending Quest

The fetus itself has two awarenesses in the womb. One is the base conscious, the awareness of the base soul. This level of consciousness acts similarly to the mind, except that it does not labor under the mind's physical constraints. As the mind develops, the base conscious becomes less the focal point of active consciousness. By age two, the mind is sufficiently developed to perform most tasks of guiding the body. The body itself has the second form of fetal awareness. The senses of the developing nervous system react to its environment, which extends beyond the womb. The nervous state of the mother, conditions of nourishment, surrounding noises and other environmental influences all affect in major or minor ways the growing biological organism. It is, after all, alive. It is the interaction between the generic characteristics of the soul and body which forms the unique awareness of the individual. The result is the elemental mind, which will be the dominant guiding force of the body for most of the waking life. The interaction of body and soul actually creates the characteristics of the mind, which can be enhanced or harmed by environmental influences.

The base soul is therefore not always a dominating consciousness. While in flesh, the base soul often appears dormant, though it never really is. It just functions in ways that the mind is in many ways oblivious of. The mind controls many waking actions, most of which are stimulated either by the base soul or the needs of the biological body. The interface point between mind and body is the brain, which gathers the impulses of the body and is in return stimulated by the physical activity of the thinking mind. The mind directs it to lift an arm, eat or resist the desire. Much of the human mind's activity is simply response to the needs and whimsies of the corporeal body. If the body's needs are satisfied, which civilization allows to be easily done, then the mind is free to pursue other habits. These other habits, though collectively building a great civilization, are usually

The Soul

also quite petty, such as fashioning or purchasing pretty adornments for the body or amusing the mind.

Despite all the wasted mental space, so to speak, there is much achieved by the soul's association with the human body. Every action is a learning process and the soul is indulging in as much learning as possible. That is man's great step forward over the other animals: he has learned how to propel his evolution using processes of the mind rather than simply allowing biological evolution to push him forward. Eventually, the soul evolves to the point where it finds the productivity of the human body in terms of good learning experience to be dropping off; at that point, usually at the close of a male incarnation, the soul moves on to a higher world. The human bodies that served that evolutionary process merely break down into atomical elements and compounds, humus to serve the soil. The minds that were associated with each of those human incarnations were one by one incorporated into the base soul to build a greater base for learning in the next life. Finally, all the carefully engineered evolution of the soul pays off and, in a manner similar to that laid out in Buddhist philosophy, the soul joins a higher world where it indulges far more efficiently in the learning process.

The human body, therefore, is a vehicle for evolution and no more. It serves a soul and in doing so creates the life-energy that is the raw material for the soul's evolution. Food energy is transformed by the body into life-energy and life-energy is transformed by the soul into soul-energy. Each incarnation during that long, cyclical process of evolution has certain goals and responsibilities: its purpose is to foment a particular type of learning. The soul itself during consolidation determines what type of learning process is to be embarked upon next. It measures and evaluates the learning and successes of the preceding incarnation and adds that knowledge to its greater collage of experience. New experiences will have been added, but most are developments of prior themes of learning.

The soul's endeavors in terms of learning are broad. Though a particular incarnation may be devoted to chemical science, the soul's broader goal may be to study atomical matter. The learning experiences of each life also do much to enhance the general wisdom of the soul. No human lives without learning more about functioning as part of a society. The interrelation of individuals is a very important facet in the soul's evolution. As all living entities must fit into the natural scheme of life, they must learn how to survive within that framework with as little negative disruption to others as possible. That simple truth relates to the fundamental principle of Karma, which can be stated as simply as Newton's Third Law of Physics: "For every action, there is an equal and opposite reaction". Every action in life has its necessary repercussions: harm, above all, causes further harm to be done.

There is a natural relationship between memory and experience, both of which are related to the natural forces of life. Both life- and soul-energy retain memories, building a base of experience on which to build a greater evolution. As the human being goes about his daily life, his life-energy structure, the Spirit, incorporates the experiences encountered as mind memories. These memories can be called back to mind through the mysterious mechanisms of will. The memories are actually incorporated into the life-energy structure, the energy forming itself around the memories, re-altering its configuration as the mind calls back another memory. The number of memories, therefore, are limited only by the number and type of experiences an individual may have during one incarnation. Once that incarnation is complete, the life-energy with its many memories is incorporated into the base soul as the permanent soul-memories of that incarnation. The soul-energy then retains

The Soul

these memories, and those of all past lives, in much the same way as does life-energy. The human mind in a future incarnation can break through to these memories with some training and recall them nearly as easily as the mind recalls memories of the present incarnation. Once formed as a soul-memory, the memory is permanent. It may not be erased unless there is some unknown force which can tear the soul apart. Memories of the mind, though relatively safe, are not indestructible before being consolidated.

Because the conscious experiences of life are screened through the mind, the soul's memories are ultimately oriented to the initial perception. Thus, if the soul perceives something directly by circumventing the sensory perceptions of the corporeal body, its memory will be that direct perception. However, if the soul gathers experiences through a body, which requires the intermediate stage of life-energy, the memories will be screened through that perception. Life-energy, like the soul, can also circumvent the corporeal body's perceptions through the phenomena we have come to describe as Extrasensory Perception. ESP, as it is popularly called, provides much of the fuel for religious belief, sorcerer's magic and mystic revelation. Once harnessed, as we humans could and should do, ESP could become a valuable tool for perception and learning. In the meantime, we rely on our sensory perceptions for most of our in-flesh memories. If we see normally, then we rely to a great extent on visual memories, though these memories are subject to the "tricks" of the mind during the perception and the eventual distortion of memory. Once remembered, an image can be called again and again into the conscious mind until the soul and Spirit separate from the flesh. At that point, the consolidation process commences and the life-energy memories are in turn incorporated into the soul as soul-memories. Some, of course, are stripped away, as souls say, by the act of using energy to catalyze the consolidation process. Most are retained and only the less worthy are dropped.

Because the mind during in-flesh life screens the bulk of perceptions, the soul submerges itself to the role of unseen guide. Its impulses, although not strictly those of intellectual thought, do force their way into the mind's consciousness to be acted upon by the mind's reason. In other words, an impulse from the soul, like a timed prompt, will stimulate a thought or action. The waking mind will be largely unaware of the source of this compulsion and usually acts unthinkingly in that general direction. However, the mind may confuse the notion or act contrarily to the soul's desire, and thus cause some problems in interpretation. That reality, although potentially damaging, is one of the disadvantages of our biological organization. The mind, because it acts semi-autonomously, cannot fulfill every objective of the soul. The interface between mind and soul is imperfect, a guarded interval between one type of primary influence and another. This interval is called the middle conscious and is similar to the barrier between the conscious mind and the subconscious mind as described in analytical psychology. It is a greater force, however, and acts principly as a control to keep the vast source of life that is the soul from overwhelming the fragile human mind.

The mind itself can peak its energies and focus its concentration in breaking through to the soul's awareness.* If this is done, there is a great deal of danger to the mind. It may not be willing to accept all the truths so discovered

---

*In effect, it was this concentration of energy that allowed me to break through to my own soul, the relationship which has allowed me to write this book. I have therefore learned to control to some extent my mind's reactions to soul impulses and have trained myself to perceive the impulses generated by other living entities. Neither the relationship with my soul nor other living entities is uncommon in human society; it occurs often but is usually unrecognized by the conscious mind for what it is. If in-flesh humans trained their children to be far more open-minded, there would be greater strides forward by the human intellect.

The Soul

— many of the teachings of its society will be proved wrong. The mind, a biased construct of the human being, may use its will to shut out the truth and adhere to its cherished though false or misleading beliefs. Its interface point with the soul, the middle conscious, again closes over and, like a porous curtain, selects only those impulses from the soul which will fit conveniently into the mind's preconceived notions.

The mind itself assimilates the information given to it by the corporeal senses but does not succeed to the extent that the soul does in learning from it. Much too often, the mind learns a truth and rejects it because the truth has no immediate relevance. That truth, however, lays dormant in the unconscious for as long as necessary and then reasserts itself when the time is right. The mind, therefore, acts as a control mechanism over what is immediately relevant. The soul, with the subconscious mechanisms of the mind, then works out what is left for the future. The memories are harbored, each striving in its own way to make the individual stronger in knowledge and wiser in action. It is best, therefore, to pay heed to the natural instincts that seem to guide your activities.

The mind is also an interface mechanism to the brain and corporeal organism. As stated earlier, it is the mind and supporting life-energy structure that bridges the alien natures of the soul and corporeal body. With the mind in ascendency, the body has some control over its immediate survival. Although it is to the soul's best advantage to retain a body for the gathering of experience, it is fully aware of when that body will be shed. The mind must be kept blissfully unaware of that moment for as long as possible. If not, the organism becomes preoccupied with imminent death, awaiting that moment without rest. Too much energy is wasted in trying to circumvent the inevitable and the soul's objectives become lost in the struggle to maintain the survival of the flesh. Whatever the individual's personal notions of what death means, he must be aware that it means great changes in his circumstances. Whether hopeful or fearful, the knowledge of the coming event will indubitably influence the individual's thinking from that point forward. For most tasks of the soul, such an awareness is an inconvenience and obstruction: resolution of the body's death is best left until necessary, at least in light of man's current understanding of the soul. When the mind is fused with the base soul upon separation from the flesh, the mind, as an individual consciousness, begins to melt away. It is methodically incorporated into the base material of the soul, becoming as integral to the primary nature of life as is possible. When the consolidation is complete, the incarnation has truly ended. In that sense, death is real.

While in flesh, however, the mind has its moment. It is ascendent for most of the waking hours, the soul secluded in the lower reaches of consciousness. The mind concentrates primarily on the signals it receives from the corporeal body, using and directing the body in the gathering of experience. Naturally, the needs of the body, mind and soul act both in harmony and in conflict, depending on the circumstances of the moment. The degrees of harmony or conflict often determine the individual's success in chosen pursuits. The soul, forced as it is to depend on the physical realities of corporeal existence, must make do with what it has. Thus, the unavoidable event of eating can be turned into a pleasant and enjoyable learning experience. It provides essential food energy in a social context, a source of both corporeal well-being and many useful experiences.

In gathering experiences from the corporeal body, the mind must use its natural sensory mechanisms in whatever state they exist. The brain, as a centralizing organ for the nervous system, provides a mechanism through which the mind can gather impressions. These impressions are then

The Soul

stored in the life-energy as memories until either called back by the mind or incorporated into the base soul. The interrelationship of the mind and brain, however, is far different than currently envisioned by scientists. For the most part, scientists think of the brain as being the seat of consciousness, when it is really only a complex organ that controls sensory activity. When stimulated by the mind, a separate entity in itself, the brain produces the electrical and chemical activity that scientists have so far observed. This activity, far from being evidence of thought itself, is the result of thought. The life-energy motivated by thought is directed to the appropriate nerve points which stimulate activity. In this sense, the mind acts like the tiny electrodes of the brain researcher: by stimulating various points in the brain, natural responses occur.

To draw a visual analogy of this process, picture a hand calculator. This calculator has all the components required to make it work: buttons, casing, electronic circuits and supporting material. It does not work without the presence of electricity and even then does nothing until guided by an intelligence, a human pressing the buttons. The human organism is analogous to the calculator. It has appendages and material which define its physical existence, a brain which provides a patterned design of circuitry with specific capabilities, and energy to make it work. It, too, requires intelligence or it is useless. For the human being, intelligence is the product of a trained mind functioning on its natural attributes. This mind is directed in its work by a base of consciousness which determines its level of wisdom in surface level decision-making. As these various levels of consciousness interact with the biological organism, chemical and electrical activity results. The body receives its direction from the mind or soul, or mind and soul acting together. Alone, the body can do nothing but decompose. Guided by a living force, however, it can perform wondrous mechanical feats.

Current scientific theory allows little room for causes of consciousness other than measured patterns of electrical and chemical activity of the brain. However, these patterns are the offshoots of consciousness, not its physical causes. Therefore, science has yet to validate any theory of intelligence, life or soul. The mistake lies in the concentration on atomical forces, when the life-force of the human being is not atomical at all. It merely cohabits with the atomical nature of the biological organism. Thus, all atomically based activity in the human body is entirely nonliving. One molecule is as dead as the next. Yet together, the molecules of the human body function in a macroscopic manner that is evidently alive, misleading some of the greatest human minds in the quest for the root of life. Only when fused with the genuine living properties of soul-energy can the body live. The soul itself lives only because of the way in which it is constructed. It can therefore incorporate nonliving matter (energy matter, that is) into itself in a particular way and become a greater unit of life. The body aids this process as it provides the first few steps in recombining simple energies into more complex energies. The body cannot, however, complete this task and that is why the body in itself and by itself cannot live.

The soul *can* live by itself. It does so during the period it spends in the Afterlife consolidating experiences and awaiting a new body. It knows it must eventually join another body but this moment can be put off for a long time. There is no real danger of the soul fading away if there is no suitable body immediately available: the post-consolidation phase is the most stable point of the cycle of reincarnation. In most cases, however, the soul does want to join another body, for that is the only way it can actively progress. In other terms, the soul may await and plan its next move indefinitely but until it actually steps daringly forward to do something, it stays essentially where it is. At

The Soul

times, the soul may develop a near-mania for progression, the hunger a very palpable force. If that influence shows up during the incarnation in flesh, the individual will be driven to achieve, perhaps beyond his ability to endure. Thus, there is much cause for illnesses resulting from an over-anxious soul. Likewise, there are many inherent weaknesses in the available bodies. For these two reasons, and others, the soul must choose very carefully the body it will use next. If it defines its immediate goals with care and executes its strategy wisely, it can push itself forward greatly.

The corporeal body to a large extent determines what the soul can achieve in a given lifetime. It will never achieve all it desires but it may certainly do well. Overall, the soul's objective is to put the body and its time in it to good use. Because life is fundamentally self-protective and self-centered, much of the effort expended is for the self. Yet the soul should also be interested in the well-being of those around it, from the most minute lifeform to the greatest. Harmony enhances the evolution of all living beings and efforts to improve the lives of others inevitably improve the life of the self. That is Karma. Thus, it is not so bad to be self-interested, as long as the self-interest does not cause undue harm to others. Each individual has the responsibility to determine what he can do and when he can do it. Often, the spiritual philosophies of man point out that the poor man who gives his last dollar away is more wealthy than a millionaire. Yet we mustn't forget that the millionaire who gives many dollars away does much more good for others. In short, there is an opposite face on every coin. The soul, as it plots its course in evolution, finds it must steer very carefully. The imperfections of a body, a world, a time or itself may make it impossible to achieve what it desires. The quest of the soul, like man's, is unfulfilled.

The study of the soul is the study of the motivations

and purposes of very complex lifeforms. The soul is not like a beating heart which may be replaced by carefully engineered plastic and the organism will still live. It is life itself. Thus, the quest for the soul has two faces: one for its material existence, which does not greatly stir the breast of science (so far), and the second for the spiritual (in the general sense) benefits of knowing the self better. The closer in harmony these fundamental quests are, the greater fulfillment will result. In fact, many people throughout the world are suffering from the encroachment of scientific fact upon theological interpretation of reality. The result is confusion, both for individuals and societies, and social turmoil. Instead of getting comfort and guidance in religion, many people are turned away by religious tenets which do not allow acceptance of scientific facts. Others find themselves of two minds: one frame of reference is used for interpretation of religious truth and another for scientific truth. The conflicting points of view in such a case are not resolved but merely placed in terms acceptable to the mind. Carl Gustave Jung wrote at great length of how unresolved issues can be shifted into the depths of consciousness. This area he called the "unconscious". Essentially, from the point of view of the surface mind, that is correct. Yet from the point of view of the soul, the condition is a vast inhibiting factor to emotional and intellectual development: it is not "unconscious" at all, but a very real and very conscious problem.

To study the soul effectively, there must be a model from which to work. Jung and his associates worked out a preliminary model of consciousness which serves as an introduction to some major conditions. The model, however, does not extend far enough in physical terms to pin down the actual structure of consciousness: it does not define the soul. While the term "ego" provides a point of reference, it does not explain what comprises such a thing. It merely

The Soul

describes a state of consciousness which can affect a person's health and well-being. A more modern branch of psychology, physiological psychology, is trying to find the physical root of consciousness but is focusing on the corporeal body. These researchers are making healthy progress in defining the human nervous system but have failed to find the root of life. Nor are they likely to, as they are looking in the wrong place, or to be more precise, they are looking at the wrong type of matter. If these researchers were to join forces with particle physicists, who are toying with the edges of atomical reality, they would soon discover many of the principles which allow the soul to interact with the body. The discovery of the soul itself would then not be far behind.

The merging of disciplines is essentially the approach I have taken in writing this book. My intent is to provide a bird's-eye view of a complex subject. As the material presented here is primarily of a very general nature, it provides a model which can be used to establish a coherent course of action. Then, as research techniques evolve, more facts will flesh out these very bare bones. In my opinion, the failure of modern psychical research to discover the governing rules of ESP and psychokinesis is that psychical researchers are not working from a model. Without a conceptual paradigm of what they want to study, the nonsensory forces of human consciousness, they have little chance for success. To illustrate this, consider the fact that although the atom was only studied in any detail beginning in the 20th Century, the original model of the atom was introduced in the 4th Century B.C. The Greek philosopher Leucippus and his pupil Democritus conceived of an indivisible particle they called the atom as being the basis of all existence. We have applied that term to the basic matter of our plane, which we have since learned is not indivisible. However, without the original model, the chances of discovering the atom would have been remote: the

Man's Unending Quest

discovery would not have come until somebody *did* create a model. The creation of even an imperfect model of a primary element of reality led to the discovery of the atom and the development of further models of other even smaller elements of reality.

By the same token, the discovery of the base matter of the soul will take a long time. Though man may never find the root of matter, he can and will find the root of life, the soul. Even if the spiritual questions of man, so dominant in his thinking for thousands of years, don't lead him to the answer, particle physics will. The soul consists of particles so tiny that the particles of the atom are gigantic by comparison. In fact, these particles may not even be particles, merely behaving in similar patterns. Be that as it may, the quest for the root of matter will inevitably cross that of the quest for the root of life. The two exist on the same continuum. Man merely approaches the point from two directions. If one course fails, the other will succeed. Yet if joined, the two courses could lead to the discovery far sooner and thus benefit man sooner. The most significant benefits would be the further development of social accord, lessening of war and enhancement of individual lives. These are the truths which man's spiritual philosophies have been teaching all along. They are just as true today. When fitted within a truer perspective of what the human being is, they will be all the more forceful and probably more effective.

The writings of man, whether scientific treatise or ancient religious text, are products of the soul. It is the soul which desires to enlighten and inform and which sparks the desire to learn. The longevity of such texts as the Bible indicates a great appeal to the human consciousness. To read, therefore, is to bring yourself closer to an understanding of the soul. The more you read from a wider range of sources, the more likely you will form a balanced perspective of life. Conversely, if you restrict your studies

The Soul

to one primary area, you will find your perspective incredibly biased. After wide reading, many common denominators emerge. These are the common denominators of human consciousness, the truths which form the basis of human society. The greatest truth to emerge from such a survey is soon obvious. That is to love. Man's first effort, above all else, should be to love, for that is his key to progress. If life on earth is truly to be improved, which is the object of all human effort, it must be through love. That is what the human soul really wants to learn about.

2

HUMANITY'S PURPOSE

Humanity is a complex collection of souls gathered in a common purpose — that of improving the soul-race Humanity. As a race of souls, Humanity extends beyond the four billion souls of human beings currently striding the face of the earth. It also includes the two billion and more souls of the Human Afterlife, who are taking their rest following incarnations in human flesh. We all go to this Afterlife when we die, regardless of our world experience, because we are a part of a shared environment that demands certain physiological responses. At times this response requires the absence of the corporeal body and though we humans often form emotional attachments to these bodies, they are really no more than vehicles for our evolution.

The soul does evolve. Each individual soul began its existence at a finite point in the past and will continue to evolve long into the future. There are no points at which evolution stops, though there are temporary points of "stasis", resting points where progression seems temporarily halted. These points are important in the reorganization of the entity's evolutionary course, and have many characteristics and types. They may be long or short, major or minor. In all cases, the finite objective is the consolidation of a purpose and the extension of a goal. Even the longest period of stasis, however, pales in comparison with the duration of the soul's environment, the realm in which the soul is evolving.

Life within the biological classification of man, the so-called human race, is merely an extension of our existence as part of the soul-race Humanity. The soul-race uses a capitalized H to denote the entire collection of human souls, in flesh and out, whereas the lower case h designates only those human beings living on the atomical earth. While in flesh, we do not often see the other side of our souls' awareness, the side which faces the Afterlife. Our awareness is like a two-sided coin, one side facing our in-flesh existence, which supports the mind, and the other side facing the world of the soul. Our souls can indeed communicate with other souls when our minds "aren't looking". The mind is usually oblivious to impulses received or sent by the base soul. If these impulses are in some way received by the mind, they are filtered through the middle conscious (as described in Chapter 1), the protective layer of consciousness that protects the mind from being overwhelmed by the greater awareness of the soul. The mind, therefore, is not overtaxed in "guessing" the soul's every purpose, something it might otherwise try to do.

The mind forms its own frame of reference around its experiences. It is guided by both soul and body but usually responds first to the needs of the body. When those needs (and many whims) are satisfied, the mind may heed more direction from the inner self. This inner self (the base soul) guides most waking actions to some degree but makes its presence felt in varying degrees of strength at different times. It rarely forces the mind to cohere to its predefined plan, though it may do so if the plan is of great enough significance. The dichotomy of soul and mind is two levels of being interacting, one complementing the other in mutual desires. Thus, when occasion calls for the wants and needs of one to be satisfied, the other must accede. If the other does not accede, the price is inner conflict, a subject familiar to psychologists. In most everyday life, however, the needs of the corporeal body are the foremost concern, because this body is the vehicle for gathering experience. Without it, the incarnation ends and so does the opportunity to learn lessons only that body could provide. Because the corporeal senses are primarily used for the ratification of experience, the less sensory-oriented perceptions can usually be ignored. Sometimes, however, nonsensory perceptions can't be ignored and the terms of interaction between mind and soul may change dramatically. Perceptions of nonsensory character, though not as common during in-flesh life as sensory perceptions, do occur. When they do, the individual is often forced to have some faith in a field of existence beyond the sensory.

As a general rule, people do not accept perceptions which do not fit their rigid interpretations of reality. In other words, each of us has a self-defined (and socially defined) version of reality that can be called "accepted reality". Thus, in modern industrial societies, it is readily accepted if a dog is seen chasing a cat into bushes. Yet it is not so readily accepted if a man appears and then disappears into thin air. Logically, however, the dog and cat could be hallucinations as easily as the man appearing and disappearing. And conversely, if both are seen under equivalent circumstances, both could be equally real. It is just the individual's sense of reality, instilled by years of experience and social training, which determines what will be believed more readily. That experience and training, however, does not preclude the experience of something totally new to that individual.

Often, people do see or experience something which does not fit into their perception of the scheme of things. When that happens, they more often suspect they are at fault themselves than immediately accept the phenomenon. To accept it would mean throwing out many years of preconceptions, something most (if not all) people are loathe to do. Many uncommon phenomena, including apparitions, clairvoyance, precognition and telepathy, have been liberally documented over the years in books as widely varied as the Bible and those which line the bookshelves in the occult sections of bookstores. One book that provides a collage of such phenomena is *The Hidden Spectre*, by Robert Tralins (see reading list). Tralins includes a list of contacts for the vignettes he presents so that the skeptical can do a little checking. In my experience, I have met many people who have had experiences similar to many of those Tralins presents and I presume any substantial gathering of people would yield a few more. All this documentation and testimony is circumstantial evidence, of course, but the sheer vast quantity of it is very convincing for those people willing to be convinced.

The human being often demands unreasonable proof of something that contradicts one of his beliefs. He much more readily accepts things which support his point of view or which at least don't contradict it. Although societies have, as a whole, accepted many, many phenomena that remain unproved, they usually do so out of religious conviction or long-standing habit. Another society may well consider the belief to be absurd and will find the compliment returned with respect to some of its own beliefs. In other words, truth is often in the eye of the beholder, especially when in regards to anything that cannot be immediately verified with the corporeal senses. Once comfortable with a set of beliefs, the individual or society is only pried away from it with very great effort over a long period of time. Proof, therefore, becomes more a state of mind than a state of fact. For example, the classic definition of proof, René Descartes' statement "I think, therefore I am" is really not proof of anything. It is an assumption: a more truthful statement would be "I think, therefore I must assume I am". In that very real sense, nothing is truly proved. Everything, including one's own existence, is based on faith. The saving grace, however, is that there are degrees of faith. There is blind faith, such as that a fundamentalist Christian places in his God, and there is reasoned faith, based on empirical studies, such as that of the realm of science. Science's definition of proof depends on the analysis of consistency. If something appears so consistently under similar circumstances that it is a certainty, then we say it is proved. If it is not easy to replicate the experience, then proof is wanting.

For most people, encountering the unproved phenomena associated with the soul (say, a ghost-like apparition or things that go bump in the night), is a matter to be feared. It is not readily accepted because it is not a part of everyday conscious experience. Yet there are people who do live with such phenomena as daily experiences: these people are usually called mediums. Although I have had many mediumistic experiences, I do not consider myself a medium. To me, a medium is a person with a natural ability far beyond the usual to contact the other levels of life. In fact, I believe the greatest value of my work is in the fact that I have only the usual level of ability in this area and that any other serious scholar should be able to repeat what I have done. Accepting the soul's existence is the first step in discovering its unexplained abilities. I don't mean here an acceptance of it in the religious sense, but an acceptance of it as a physical thing, like the body is a physical thing. Granted, the religious perception of the soul originally treated it as a real thing but many modern thinkers tend to think of it as a figurative concept only. The soul, to them, is a quality of consciousness, defined in abstract terms as we would define the "character" of an architectural structure. In a sense, these thinkers are like Columbus' contemporaries who believed in the flatness of the world: to them, it didn't matter that Eratosthenes some 1800 years before had proved that the earth was spherical; all that mattered was their conventional belief.

The greatest single hurdle in proving the soul's existence (or any other essentially nonsensory phenomenon) is the lack of tangible evidence. In the introduction, I described how I sometimes have strikingly accurate precognitive dreams. If I denied having these inexplicable dreams of the future, I would only be lying to myself, not the world. Yet people often tell me that I could not have experienced such a thing because it doesn't fit into *their* interpretation of the world. If they have decided something is impossible, no amount of testimony on my part will convince them that I have indeed experienced something that proves their restricted view of the world to be inadequate. In spite of our hindsight which tells us that no society has ever yet achieved a perfect view of our environment, we still hope or sometimes even believe that we have achieved such a perfect view. That, perhaps, is the product of a technological society which has opened up frontiers of knowledge many past societies could not even imagine. More likely, however, it is the product of human conceit.

Belief aside, human imagination often seems to be the precursor of real knowledge. If we imagine something, we usually find some basis in truth for it. H.G. Wells wrote science fiction stories about travelling to the moon when even atmospheric flight was relatively untried. Although people claimed such travel was impossible (as they did atmospheric flight), modern technology has exceeded the fiction. Yet the average skeptic from the Western world will abruptly reject a notion (the existence of the soul) that has thousands of years of history and documented belief because he cannot perceive the soul with his senses. Despite increasing empirical evidence that a life-force exists within the human body that survives the body's death, the skeptic refuses to

Humanity's Purpose

accept the *possibility* that there may be a soul. But if we mounted an unfettered exploration of the soul, we would explain many human experiences science has to date been unable to come to terms with.

No investigation has caused as much confrontation and suffering as the quest for the human soul. Holy wars and conquest have raged throughout the world for thousands of years, the result of one group or another forcing their neighbors to accept their doctrines. In essence, in seeking to learn of the guiding forces of the soul, man creates religions which he often takes far too seriously. Even today, it seems as though science deliberately purges the word soul from its vocabulary. Perhaps vestiges of witch hunts and Inquisitions remain: at one time, to disagree with the standing order of Christianity, the dominant religion in the areas in which modern science emerged, was to invite torture and death. Science instead prefers the terms psyche (Greek for soul), mind, ego and even "electro-chemical impulses" to refer to the stuff of life. Yet none of these terms addresses the heart of the matter. They are labels as good as any other for *aspects* of the life process, but do not describe life itself. To discover life is one of the great purposes of science, yet scientists steer away from the greatest concept of life: the soul.

Partly, scientists fear to tread on ground deemed religious. To do so often brings public ridicule on themselves for being "unscientific", just because of the choice of subject matter and irrespective of the methodology used. Thus, many scientists find safer ground in exploring the rings of Saturn, searching deeper into the world of quarks or developing a detergent that whitens and brightens better than before. This is not to say that all scientists should focus their efforts on the soul, for interests are widely varied. Yet there should not be the blatant prejudice against areas that until recently man could only deal with through religion. The soul is not just a religious concept or an occult theme. Its metaphysical reality should not override its physical reality. The soul is a very real aspect of the physical universe and should be treated as such; it should be given all the unbiased attention that science can muster. Although many scientists feel that to touch upon matters traditionally regarded the province of priests and mystics is to invite ridicule, they should not be so afraid. Peer pressure is a sad reality that all of us must face but we need not succumb to it. It is the far-reaching ideas of men such as Galileo and Darwin who thrust man's knowledge into the future. Sadly, both these men were forced to retract certain ideas in the face of peer pressure (in Galileo's case, at the threat of burning at the stake) that were later proved correct.

Man has never learned to adapt himself to the revelation of truth. The standing order always attacks and denounces any theory that strays too far from favored central themes or forces too much revision of accepted ideas and doctrine. This is as true today as ever before. Of course, there are ample examples of crackpot theories that remain crackpot theories, but enough "crackpot" theories have later proved to be right that we should be far more tolerant of ideas that are new or different. Darwin gives us an example that is still the center of controversy. When his theory of evolution was first presented in the mid-19th Century, many Christians regarded it as absurd, holding instead to Christian doctrine of Creation. In the intervening century, the tables have turned. The holdouts of fundamentalist Christian belief that the universe was created in six days (seven, counting the day of rest) in 4004 B.C. are now regarded as a fringe element. Darwin's basic theory has been proved valid.*

---

*Any Creationist who still refuses to accept Darwin's principle theory of evolution has either failed to understand the concept or is refusing to face reality. Everything evolves and evidence for evolution is everywhere you look. If you want to see evolution at work, just look at any garden with its genetically engineered flowers

Humanity's Purpose

Despite the failings of the interpretations of many old legends, all contain some truth, even if that truth is an imaginary combination of several real experiences. Consider the Minotaur, the half-bull, half-human of classical mythology. Obviously, such a beast is not a plausible arrangement of biomass but is instead the imaginary combination of two realities, a human being and a bull. The imaginary entity is not real in itself but is derived from real experiences of the people who came up with the idea. All imagination is similarly based in genuine facts and experiences, no matter how much reality is in the end distorted. If there was no real experience to distort, no distortion would take place. In other words, the mind needs something known to imagine something previously unknown. Finite experience is the foundation for everything imagined.

Thus, man's mythologies and legends, however illusory and misleading they may be in a quest for facts, can provide much fuel for any search for truth. They may not be true as written or told but are definitely based on real experiences. The challenge, therefore, is to eke out the facts and accurate truths amongst the imaginary reconstructions. Such a discipline can be based on the analysis of reality according to consistency, the same basic method of any scientific endeavor. Every scientist searches for truth on that basis: if consistent action begets consistent reaction, then a law is at work. That scientific principle, though honed and disciplined into a remarkable tool, is based on nothing other than the human animal's need to identify factors in its environment to better enable it to survive. Everything learned is learned according to that method. Science merely idealizes

---

or vegetables. Even our philosophies evolve, including those that the Christian Creationists claim as their absolute source: the Bible. Within that text, the teachings of the entity called God evolved from Genesis to Revelation. Christ's teachings, for instance, are far more liberal than the Laws of Moses. Time has wrought great changes in all things, including man's ideas.

it and establishes criteria which mean truths so discovered cannot be easily refuted.

When analyzed on that basis, mythology and religion provide many consistent truths which can be taken as some indication of something real. One of these universal constants is the human belief in the soul. All societies have evolved a mythology of human existence which includes reference to a human spiritual quality which transcends the corporeal body and atomical plane. In addition, man conceives of a universal destiny in his religions and other philosophies which places him under the guidance of higher intelligences and subject to the whims of many other-worldly entities. Although he calls these entities gods, spirits, ghosts, demons, fairies, nymphs, angels, elfs and devils, he maintains remarkably consistent views of life beyond his known realm. Although it is possible that any of these mythological entities, be they gods or lesser spirits, are falsely presented in human mythology (to which the legends of all religions belong), it does not necessarily mean there are no entities which may have sparked such belief. In other words, if all imagination is based in fact, what facts led to these mythologies? There must be a common denominator at work and though the skeptic would say it is human imagination, I counter that imagination would struggle to create from nothing concepts as complex as the soul or other worlds.

There are other worlds. That this is true is evident in all of the human experience: we just have to capture enough of that experience in scientific terms to come to some understanding of it. When that happens, the existence of other worlds within the sphere of this planet will not be denied any more than we now deny the existence of air. Even now, to deny the existence of the soul is to damage your ability to control your effects on your environment, which extend to these other worlds. As a species, man cannot afford to hide from these worlds. If he does, he may do

Humanity's Purpose

irreparable damage to his own future.

The failure of modern man to fully define the truths of his historical teachings leaves him at the mercy of his own misunderstanding of his "realm of effect". Unless he fully understands how he affects his environment, he cannot control that effect. Naturally, some effects boomerang, causing him much harm, sometimes without his even knowing he is the ultimate cause of the repercussion. As every individual element of the universe affects all other elements, human actions can theoretically be felt to the end of time. In human terms, your most immediate realm of effect is your immediate society: your friends, family and social structure. As you interact with your society, your realm of effect spreads ever outwards like the ripples of a stone cast into water. It is therefore to your advantage to understand as much as possible the effects of your every action, even though you cannot possibly know *all* the effects. This process of understanding leads to greater control of your own life, though never complete control. As you improve your perceptions and your understanding, you learn more about their effects and extend your "realm of reference".

Your realm of reference is merely your perception of your place in the universe. It differs from your realm of effect in that it relates to a perception and not an absolute. In other words, your realm of effect is ultimately the entire universe because nothing can be truly separated from the universe, but you needn't perceive that whole as a frame of reference. In fact, man perceives only a very small part of it, hardly touching the far reaches of the atomical level of the universe with his telescopes and ignoring all other worlds near at hand, such as his own Afterlife. In any event, you extend your realm of reference as you understand more and more of your interrelation with the environment. If you choose, your realm of reference may only be a few friends

Man's Unending Quest

and family members with whom you regularly associate. Or you may extend your view to a broader perspective, say a business, a neighborhood, a country or even the whole world. You can include as much in your realm of reference as you are comfortable with in terms of your shared responsibility for universal well-being. You therefore monitor your own actions and are able to govern the amount of harm you cause — because of our limited perspectives, we cause a lot of harm without realizing it.

Because of your nature as a living entity, you must survive. The very act of survival forces you to do harm either directly or indirectly to other life and facets of the environment. This harm results in what souls call "bad Karma" and must be offset by "good Karma". Thus, because of Karmic principles of cause and effect, you must ensure that your good actions far outweigh your harmful actions. Because you live, you have a right to your own "Karmic Place", your own individually modifiable realm of effect. As you can control to some degree your influence on what surrounds you, you may make every effort possible to see that your actions lead to improvements and not harm. As even the act of living interrupts the life-cycles of other entities (by using a vehicle that could be used by another, if no other reason), there is no means of ensuring that you do no harm whatsoever. That, however, is no excuse not to minimize the harm that you cause. If you eat meat, for instance, you can be certain that you share the responsibility for taking an animal's life, yet you have also provided the soul of that animal an opportunity to advance to the next phase of its life-goals.* Thus, your only aid in determining

---

*Even the most minute lifeform has a life-goal, to survive. As entities evolve, they acquire greater and greater goals, becoming more complex in their interrelationship with their environment until eventually they achieve the ability to intelligently modify that environment. Although man is the greatest modifier of environment in his atomical world to date, others, notably the beaver, nest-building birds and bees, have remarkable skills in environment-shaping.

Humanity's Purpose

what is a good action and what is harmful is to understand as much as possible the realm of effect of your actions. Mistakes in judgement can be corrected, but it is difficult to undo harm that already has been done. Much more effective is avoiding causing the harm in the first place and you can only do this by increasing your awareness. As humanity is engaged in the task of improving itself and its actions, the species must gather much more knowledge. Only through such knowledge can the essential intelligence be brought to bear on many, many problems facing the species and the planet to which it belongs.

Your potential effect on your environment is much greater than it first appears. As man has begun to realize even the tiniest of actions, such as using spray cans filled with fluorocarbon propellants, can threaten the entire biosphere of the planet. Thus, man's efforts to control his effects on his environment must stem from a vast understanding of very minute elements of that environment. He must define the interrelationship of the elements of the environment and determine how he can interact with those elements with minimum possible disruption.

Ideally, all elements of the universe should be allowed to pursue their own destinies unmolested, whether living or nonliving. Of course, since the universe continually evolves, this ideal is impossible to achieve. Rather, all elements of the universe *continually* disrupt each other in an infinity of ways. The achievable task of man, therefore, is to control as much as he can his interaction with the other elements of the universe and thereby reduce the unnecessary disruption. To do this, man must come to understand the universe and its parts, which interrelate on the basis of "functional unities". Universe, of course, is the catchword for everything that exists everywhere. Everything we can know or conceive of is a part of the universe. When we study the parts of the universe that we can perceive, we must in some way separate each part from the whole. Thus, we divide the universe into functional unities for the purposes of analysis according to the natural divisions we can perceive.

The universe that we perceive on a daily basis is primarily the atomical plane. This is an extensive plane, which extends billions of lightyears from here in all directions. This plane can be described as a functional unity based on its construction of atomical matter. Within it, there are lesser functional unities, including galaxies, solar systems and solar bodies. We give each fundamental concept a term to describe its inherent unity, a label with which to identify it. The concept of functional unity can extend to anything that functions as some form of cohesive entity. We define all our concepts, great or small, in terms of unities.

Conceptualization in terms of unities does not apply just to material entities. We classify biological organisms into taxonomic structures, with each kingdom, class, order, genus and species forming fundamental unities on a descending scale. We even raise our conceptualization to describe laws of mathematics or principles of philosophy as functional unities of thought. This grouping of substance into a coherent whole does not physically separate the subject from the universe. It merely allows the human animal to rationalize a part of the universe independently of the whole, despite the subject's dependence on the rest of the universe for its existence.

Determining what should be a functional unity, however, can be difficult. At first glance, it would seem reasonable to define a human being, for example, as a functional unit. Each human being can act as essentially a self-contained entity, given his natural interrelationship with his environment. Although he is not fully independent, it seems fair to grant him the quasi-independent status of functional unity, as we would also do for, say, an atom. But getting right down close to the human being on an

Humanity's Purpose

atomical level would make it very difficult to see that human as being in any way independent of his environment. Atoms are by no means solid nor do they have firmly defined edges. And each minute particle of each atom emits its own radiation that extends in all directions, theoretically infinitely. We can only recognize in a macroscopic manner that there is an optimum point at which to divide the human being from his environment in conceptual terms: what he sees is what he is. It is not surprising, therefore, that each individual human being does not see himself so much as a *part* of the universe but as functionally independent within it.

We humans often find the concept that our environment is actually only a physical extension of ourselves to be quite disturbing. An illustration of this reaction is the reception of Canadian philosopher Marshall McLuhan's theories of the "Extensions of Man" (from *Understanding Media*, see reading list). In McLuhan's thinking, everything in human civilization, including books, buildings and weapons, are actually a part of man. Man is not just the biological organism, in McLuhan's eyes, but everything that man has produced as well. McLuhan's ideas evoked many reactions, not all of them favorable. In recent years, his ideas have perhaps been set aside, but they did create quite a stir for a considerable time. The Western intellectual community has equal difficulty in adjusting to the concept of a soul that is at once divisible from the human body and dependent on it. The notion of external spiritual entities communicating with this soul without the medium of the body is even a greater mystery to the Western world. In the Western world, we tend to acknowledge these concepts only in the abstract or superficial terms of religion. Instead of regarding them as plausible extensions of the finite human experience, we consider them only as mythology or as matters of faith. And when matters of faith are shaken by scientific discoveries, the tendency to relegate the unknown to the wastebasket

Man's Unending Quest

of mythology is strengthened. McLuhan's ideas can't really be tested, so they are kept as a sort of intellectual curiosity. Likewise, because we haven't been able to locate the Afterlife with our corporeal senses or our manufactured machines, too many of us assume it doesn't exist.

Human societies all have notions of the spiritual life beyond this atomical plane. Unfortunately, the notions were rarely developed in intellectual terms and for the most part surfaced in the practices and precepts of religion. Although human religions have many different precepts and practices, most are molded around definable principles which can be considered universal human denominators. When separated from mythological or historical legend (especially from tales of the never-ending battles, both earthly and heavenly, that religious histories and legends have enshrined), the common tenets of religion can be summed up quite precisely. One commonality is the principle of love and aid to be shown to fellow man. This principle is expressed in Christianity, for example, as the Golden Rule: "Do unto others as you would have others do unto you". Another common principle is the establishment of moral codes to govern the behavior of the people adhering to the religion, though the nature of the codes do vary. These codes are intended to enable members of a society to live better lives and to help them interact with other members of that society. In many industrialized countries, criminal codes and secular constitutions have in part supplanted the religious codes. The most important commonality, perhaps, is that religions all establish the principles of interaction with higher worlds and the entities that live there. Religions also usually depict these higher worlds as being accessible only by the discarnate soul, not the corporeal body.

These common truths are simply the organized precepts of the soul's Karma, their universality a product of the common experience of human souls. There is no grand design laid out by any individual prophet or divinity that has instilled these truths in widely disparate human societies. Each society has found its own course and has been led by the very nature of the human beings in those societies to the same truths. Though some societies, more so now than ever before, do spread their beliefs widely, that doesn't preclude any society from arriving at similar beliefs independently. Once an idea comes into force, however, it can spread quickly. The spreading of religious truth is often embarked upon with a vicious fervor that has less than truthful results. Despite a sound core of truth in its philosophy, plus whatever individual truths a given religion or sect can add to general human knowledge, there can be a lot of other negative factors and untruths involved in any religion. Because the human being is such a jealous creature concerning his carefully cherished conceptions, he has often gone to war and administered barbaric deviations of justice to those who disagreed with him or stood in his way. Often, these actions are in direct conflict with some of the basic precepts of the beliefs in question but good philosophy does not always deter harmful actions.

Even though most of the practices of human religions are just the imaginative embellishments of core doctrine or belief, it is often the practices which garner the greatest attention. Thus, it doesn't matter that the prophets of the world's religions wished to steer mankind to greater love; mankind himself uses the localized practices established by those same prophets as a cause célebre. The classic argument between Jews and Christians has erupted into many violent confrontations since the crucifixion of Christ, the most violent being the annihilation of six million Jews by the deranged military dictator Hitler. Hitler no doubt believed his cause was just, but how wrong he was and how contrary to the basic precepts propounded by his society's dominant religion, Christianity. For even though Hitler may have been

Man's Unending Quest

the catalyst, it was indeed German society (and others) which tolerated the mass murders of not only Jews but many other people. Although these societies have become more liberal since then and many individuals more so, humankind still kills for its beliefs and still can be just as wrong.

Despite his quest into his higher nature, man seems to fear what he will find if he considers the soul and his gods as physical entities. Perhaps he is afraid in a global sense that too much revelation too fast will cause great upheaval among his societies. Despite the growing secular attitudes of modern industrial societies, there is little social grouping on the basis that there is no soul or no gods. If there is a group or society of humans organized on the basis that there is no soul, I don't know of it. Individuals who choose not to believe there is a soul often reverse this belief at some later point in life. Whatever an individual chooses to believe, he must face the issue sooner or later. We all die. For that reason, if no other, it is useful to study the forces of the human soul. In an absolute, empirical sense, the existence of life after the death of the flesh remains unproved. Yet the circumstantial evidence is overwhelming and is certainly far too great for any serious scientist (or layman, for that matter) to reject the possibility categorically. There should (and will) be an organized quest for the human soul at all levels of human endeavor. Religious texts and philosophies, however imperfect or localized, may well be the best starting place for this quest.

Much work has already been done in terms of comparative religion. An excellent work that deals with the various mythologies of religion and human society as a whole is *The Two Hands of God* by Alan W. Watts (see reading list). In this book, Watts analyzes many common traits in human mythology in light of Carl Jung's idea that the human mind produces common elements in mythology throughout the world. In reality, it is the base soul, not the

Humanity's Purpose

mind, which is the ultimate source of these commonalities in mythology but Jung's idea is otherwise correct. Through such analysis of myth, the commonalities will eventually emerge and be thoroughly catalogued. At that point, empirical studies may commence to determine what causes them to recur throughout human myth. To fully study this problem, man will need to understand more of the soul and will have to be willing to drop some of his less practical religious beliefs and define a much more logical perception of the soul. Once proved by science, the existence of the human soul and its categorized relationship to its environment would become a part of every elementary school curriculum. Acceptance of the soul, its defined properties and its ability to guide a conscious organism would then be as automatic as is the current acceptance of the existence of the atom.

Disciplined research has long been documenting irrefutable evidence of forces regarded as mystical. Much evidence exists in parapsychological research and in documented testimony of chance events that indicates there is a life-force that can transcend the corporeal body. There is also evidence that there are spiritual entities that somehow manifest themselves in our world on occasion. These spiritual entities can be described as divinities, ghosts or phantoms, but they do have a great influence on human societies. Some four billion humans currently living in flesh and billions more who lived in flesh in the past believe or have believed in various forms of mysticism, including beliefs in divinities and the soul. Can science just ignore the massive scope of this belief, when even many scientists themselves hold such beliefs? Still, science on the whole scoffs at those who try to discover what lies behind belief in gods and the soul. The notion that science should be unbiased suffers terribly in the face of the great biases of most scientists against any exploration of mystic worlds. Just as science was blocked in its infancy by religious zealots protective of their mysticism, modern scientists block development of disciplines that explore mysticism. Though the notion still runs strong that man is subject to divine guidance, science fails to search out the physical nature of that guidance. There are still notions in the scientific world that man is on the verge of defining the total universe, though his efforts only reveal new vistas to be explored. We should always remind ourselves that a century ago some scientists wanted to close the U.S. patent office because "everything had been invented".

Even in our most enlightened societies, forces are at work which would retain outmoded and inadequate theories at pain of great suffering and death. The indoctrination of a society demands strict adherence. Anything new is challenged to the point of unreasonable impedance. In many instances, societies behave like children told of cabbage leaves and storks who then discover their births are biological. The new knowledge is immediately suspected of great impracticality and is retarded or blocked by the imaginary constructs of earlier beliefs based on faith. Man's fault in not accepting new truths readily is not an inability to rationalize but an unwillingness to accept something new that destroys his cherished misconceptions. Indoctrination, therefore, is a very effective means of maintaining societal order and control of individuals within that society. If all or most individuals are vehemently protective of the society's ideas (be they religious or secular), then the dominant order in that society has little likelihood of being overthrown. Values and truth, therefore, are interpreted in light of the political and economic expediencies of the day, not in the traditional manner in which they were originally intended. It is therefore likely that all of mankind has lost sight of the original precepts laid down in his current crop of religions. He is no longer able to interpret them as they would have been interpreted when originally devised. Moral and religious truth, therefore, is lost in the shadows of local interpretation.

I suggest that it is far better to pursue an individual course of learning, be it in a religious or secular sense, for the individual may then use his own rational prowess to resolve matters of morals or doctrine. If something makes no sense whatsoever to the rational mind, it is eventually rejected anyway. The process, much like the stripping away of primitive notions concerning the cause of meteorological phenomena, is an eventual rationalization of truth. If a thunderstorm cannot be defined in any other way, it is called activity of the gods. Yet if a meteorological theory can be devised which explains it, the theory is secularized and becomes the rational explanation. The old theory of godly wars or heavenly bodies crashing into one another may take centuries to fall away or may be retained indefinitely in remote areas, but is eventually replaced. In modern terms, the industrialization of society has meant much scientific discovery has driven less practical religious ideas from the public mind. Industrialized society on the whole has become far less oriented to religion and religion has become a secondary facet of life, in some way divisible from the main occupations of the day. And there arises the modern division of Church and State.

The social repercussions of any new truth can be astronomical. Just as the industrial revolution has reorganized the world's approach to religion, and hence life itself, the discovery of the origins of religious thought would redirect it further. If the human being became fully and indisputably aware of the nature of his own soul and the forces which guide it, he would be able to dispense with the classical idea of religion and orient his quest in a far more practical way. Organized religion, already fighting a rearguard action against social progress, would find many more traditional practices to be irrelevant or impractical constructs of human imagination. A new philosophy of existence would emerge, binding all peoples through a common perception of truth. Knowledge, therefore, could proceed on the basis of absolute truth, not in the confused and self-contradictory way it often does in the human quest. As science increasingly indicates that all reality can be defined mathematically and tested empirically, man needs only to define the mathematical laws relating to the human soul and to the entities that guide it to bring him to a true understanding of human spirituality. The definition of the precepts of religions as they relate to universal truth would then become much more clear and the untrue localizations developed through ritual and misconception would fall away. There is only one Truth to the universe. That Truth is existence itself and understanding of it must be eked out bit by bit for man's greater understanding of his Karmic Place.

In much of the industrialized world, people are trained not to believe in mysticism, despite their religious teachings. This seemingly contradictory approach to life has the advantage of allowing the individual to perceive himself as part of a finite sphere which can be practically defined and yet maintain a skeptical distance from truths that do not enter the immediate environment. One such truth that can be deferred in terms of rationalization is the continuation of life after the death of the flesh. Although man has much direct testimony and experiential evidence to support this fact, many people in industrialized societies cannot accept it. Even a carefully compiled book such as that of U.S. psychologist Kenneth Ring, *Life At Death: A Scientific Investigation of the Near-Death Experience*, which categorically supports the life-after-death phenomenon as it has been described in human testimony for thousands of years, veers away from acknowledging it as fact. Instead,

Humanity's Purpose

the book uses the term "near-death experience" as a cultural pad against attack by peers who would state (perhaps rightly so) that experiential evidence doesn't prove anything. Yet the fact remains: people who are declared clinically dead and are revived often speak of a consciousness that continued. I can vouch for many of those experiences; my techniques of automatic writing and soul-contact have led me through many bizarre experiences, including astral projection and past-life recall. Not only am I certain that there is life after the death of the flesh but I can recall some between-life experiences as clearly as my memories of childhood. I cannot accept any argument that would describe these memories as any less "real" than memories of this life. If I did, I would not be able to trust my senses to perceive any truth. My ability to analyze the consistencies of my environment would thus be short-circuited and my ability to survive effectively within that environment greatly reduced.

In my efforts to understand the phenomena I have experienced, I have followed both the circuitous routes of science and religion. Neither can offer me satisfactory answers. Both are oriented to proving facets of my experience to be "unreal". It is perhaps only habit that drives man to call anything that is unknown "supernatural"; perhaps it is easier to acknowledge unexplainable events as being beyond physical reality than to acknowledge an imperfect knowledge of reality. Yet that approach can never be acceptable in a genuine search for truth and knowledge. If there is an event, there are laws that support it. If the laws currently known fail to support it, then there are more laws to be discovered. Man has yet to discover everything and no law he has yet discovered is fully defined.

Our purpose as living entities is far more than to just understand our history or to explain the inner workings of the human psyche. We only need to understand those things so that we may pursue our main tasks. If we don't understand what we are and how we have come to be as we are, how can we fulfill any mission to our fullest? We have built a large and virtually uncontrolled world community which goes to war rather than settle arguments peacefully. We prefer to control individuals within society through government rather than to control government through individuals. As governmental forces seek greater and greater forms of government, individual peoples strike out for autonomy. As humans struggle to control their collective destiny, they also struggle to maintain their individuality. This pushing and pulling is a self-made quest; there is no single authority which knows how to achieve the perfect balance and the perfect human society. Thus, our goal for a harmonious community of kindred nations is far from being achieved, even though that is part of our earthly purpose. That society can only be created out of love and understanding, the force of mutual cooperation. This cooperation is an expression of Karma; it is the force of love. Yet that expression must ultimately be a part of the efforts of each individual human soul. That is Humanity's Purpose.

3

MAN'S IMPERFECT TRUTH

Man will know no perfect truth for man's truth will always be incomplete. No matter how much knowledge he assimilates, he can never know the full truth of all the universe. His awareness is simply too restricted. Still, Man seeks the ultimate truth and knowledge of all existence. In that knowledge, he assumes, there will be some final form of stasis, some complete and total happiness that will endure forever. He selects his mythologies on that basis, sends out his scientists to discover new truths with that ever-shining grail to tempt them. Yet because the elements of the universe constantly shift, move and intermix, like water in a turning drum, man cannot know and interpret every part of the universe at every instant. That remains beyond his power and will remain beyond his power for the duration of human existence.

    Even so, our quest is not futile. We constantly improve our knowledge, even though we may be sure it won't lead Humanity to any perfect state of existence. What we learn as human beings is directly applied to the advancement of the human soul, though no truth we discover may ever be fully and purely interpreted. As a soul-race, Humanity is founded on its many members and what they are. As imperfect as they are, they comprise the total experience of the race. Although that total experience may be expected to contain some absolute and definible truth, it can never be fully pinned down because Humanity itself is not a constant force. As its members change and evolve, the truth of the race evolves and endures. At the same time, it raises new questions, develops new imperfections to be corrected, creates more understanding and pushes the realm of knowledge further into the unknown. Whatever we discover, we must assimilate; whatever we assimilate leads us further into the reaches of the universe to areas we were previously unaware of or had little understanding of. Our truth remains imperfect because we cannot learn everything there is to know simultaneously at every instant.

Though we cannot discover everything there is to know, we can achieve greater knowledge than we currently possess. That greater understanding should be the reward in itself, for it allows us to improve our collective existence and to enhance our individual evolution. As we are part of a common race, we have common goals, which we may call "ideals", or as souls say, "Godly Ideals". These common goals may be expressed in a variety of ways but can be divided according to the major principles of living existence. Life has additional properties over nonliving matter: though ultimately constructed from the same material, life has intelligence and self-direction (even if only the most minimal lifeform). As lifeforms can be divided into categories according to their level of evolution, they can be said to have achieved a certain state, though that state can never be fully and completely defined. In other words, Humanity is a defined group of some magnitude, yet it remains an active and evolving force. Thus, the goals of Humanity can be as many or as varied as the individuals within that race but maintain the cohesiveness of common intent. That common intent, as discussed in Chapter 2, is to build a greater Humanity through acts of love. Love is our Godly Ideal, the force which our race is meant to concentrate on for its own betterment.* With that experience in hand, we can be certain that we will learn more of other ideals which we find difficult to achieve on this plane.**

Our primary goal (interpreted here as the common goal of Humanity) will lead us to a higher awareness that will eventually be the basis for Human advancement to the next division, or category, of evolution in terms of soul-race. Though we cannot achieve any perfect state either as individuals or a soul-race, we can achieve better states. Our combined efforts as a species on earth will provide the foundation for the evolution of souls that will eventually join higher worlds. In other words, the race of souls we call Humanity, though essentially a cohesive collection of souls, does allow individual members to leave the race and join a higher race when ready for that experience. Similarly, other souls join Humanity from lower levels of experience as they achieve sufficient experiential evolution to allow the graduation. In short, Humanity as a collection of souls does not retain any specific membership. Souls belong to this race (and all other soul-races) according to their level and type of experience. As souls evolve at varying rates, some remain a part of Humanity through more incarnations of the flesh

---

*I do not care to argue *why* each individual should work for his own betterment and the betterment of mankind. If the moral rightness of helping rather than hurting is not self-evident, there is little point in discussing it. If, however, an individual wishes to pursue the argument of good vs. bad for intellectual fulfillment or to hone his debating skills, the ultimate results will be no more definite than to argue for or against the existence of matter. René Descartes and George Berkeley (see *Theory of Knowledge*, reading list) thrashed that out some 300 years ago. Sooner or later, everyone must recognize the fruitlessness of pursuing harmful acts, just as everyone must behave as though physical objects exist.

**One of these ideals is freedom, an ideal we think about a great deal and some of us pursue actively. Yet, because of our physical, environmental and social limitations, there is little true freedom in the human world. All freedom here is bought at great cost. Yet there are worlds where freedom as an ideal and as a practical reality can be studied much more effectively. The human soul is destined to evolve toward these worlds, which is discussed briefly in this book and will be discussed in greater detail in a future book.

than others, with others anxiously striving to achieve higher states. When those efforts are successful, as the world's religions teach, the new world can lead to great joy for the soul.

The failure of the in-flesh human being to understand the nature of these higher worlds is the result of his reluctance to abandon facets of his religious beliefs to attain the common truths told in all religions. Further, his sciences have not yet led him to a full discussion of these realities in practical terms. Because of the physical relationship of body and soul, which produces the byproduct we call mind, we have difficulty in assimilating knowledge of non-atomical worlds. The soul is fully aware of these worlds and the mind has demonstrated abilities to contact them as well. Yet the human corporeal body, based as it is on atomical principles, does not contact these worlds directly; its only interface is via the mind and the base soul, either of which may stimulate the nervous system to cause physiological reaction. These reactions are often inexplicable, if consciously noted by the mind, or ignored altogether. They occur so routinely that physiological response to stimulus by the individual's own soul or another soul is ignored as a normal facet of life.

But the mind itself may not be able to assimilate all that is happening to the human physiology. The human mind's capabilities are decidedly directed to linear thought, that is, to working out relationships in methodical point by point analysis. Because the soul functions on a much more instantaneous basis (that is, holistically), assimilation occurs without conscious rationalization. Thus, though the soul generally "knows" through its holistic interpretation of physical reality how the mind or body will react to a given stimulus, it may not be 100 percent positive. There is room for the mind to bend the body to some ulterior desire or vice versa. The mind is not a fully known quality to the soul; its abilities, though well mapped out, do retain some

Man's Imperfect Truth

individuality and decision-making capability. (In metaphysics, this is known as "free will".) Thus, the mind is the greatest unknown factor in human experience, though as you read this book it seems to be your most familiar consciousness, reflecting your in-flesh bias. Because our minds can partially shut themselves off from the awareness of the base soul, they do not know the full intent of the soul's desires for that incarnation.

The base soul when in flesh does not have absolute control over the mind. The mind, therefore, must be entrusted to make its own resolutions of events within that incarnation and, as I mentioned earlier, prefers to do so in a linear analysis of events. Naturally, this linear analysis takes a great deal more time and is far less efficient than holistic interpretation but it seems effective for generating an acceptance or understanding of reality.

In our quest for perfect knowledge, much of our effort stems from the fact that the mind seems unable to focus on holistic interpretation (which *is* one of its skills) and concentrates instead on linear analysis. If we perceive danger, for instance, we will very rapidly assimilate it and may react instinctively. That instinct to preserve the self may be described as a holistic reaction; yet at the same time, we may impose rational thought on that instinctive process, enabling us to indulge in a decision-making process. If that decision is wrong or does not emerge fast enough, we may be overtaken by the threat. Yet clearly, there is an increasing desire on the part of the in-flesh human to take decisions unto his own mind. This increasing rationalization is the result of secularized science which must empirically test all it believes. Thus, "knowledge", that temporal reality, is subjected to more serious criteria than in, say, the context of religious belief. The soul is fully aware of this increasing rationalization and takes part in it as a submerged guide. Its awareness does not necessarily force itself upon the mind but because it is the primary base of experience upon which the mind draws, its influence cannot be completely avoided.

The soul develops its goals for a given incarnation during the consolidation phase in the Afterlife. It decides what direction the next life is to take and even decides the major elements of that life. It decides, for instance, when major life-events such as marriage will occur and how death may come, if these factors are crucial to the soul's immediate goals. These events are not chance, as many secularly oriented humans believe. They are the result of a careful analysis by the soul of all the events surrounding a given incarnation. Though this analysis is done holistically, it is not done without intelligence; the soul simply uses a different rationalization process than linear analysis. Thus, the soul decides first what it wishes to achieve, then sets about analyzing the events of the future to discover possible means of achieving them. It must first select a vehicle, a body, and the appropriate social circumstances. The soul does face certain constraints in making its decisions; much is done according to what is available. Yet the soul may also wait for the appropriate moment in time, when a suitable body (each human body provides indisputable advantages and skills over others) and set of social circumstances emerge. Often forced to compromise, the movements of people and shifting focuses of in-flesh life often indicate the careful nurturing of long-term goals by souls. The soul is aware that it must build its experience carefully. Mistakes are costly because life cannot be repeated, only begun afresh in new circumstances.

Each step in the soul's progress is measured against its ultimate goals. Because it is a part of a human society, it must further the common goals of that society. It must also react to the physiological stimuli it faces and bear the risk of making intellectual mistakes during in-flesh life when the mind may have full ascendency. As each element of exper-

Man's Imperfect Truth

ience is satisfactorily completed, the soul uses that base as a springboard to gain further desirable experiences. As all experience adds to the overall consciousness of the soul, the elements of experience gathered should ideally be as central to the goals of the soul as possible. When sidetracked, the soul only loses time and definition in its quest.

Because each incarnation is a definite step in an evolutionary progression, the planning stage is of the utmost importance. If factors of the coming incarnation are not correctly interpreted, then major setbacks may result. Each incarnation has a formative influence on the personalities of subsequent incarnations. Failures lead to unhappiness and unhappiness sets a poor stage for further positive development. In essence, your life maintains its current course primarily because of previous incarnations you don't consciously remember. Your soul is aware of that history, however, and seeks very much to correct past mistakes and add to its overall quest. It cannot ensure, however, that certain mistakes won't be repeated under the management, shall we say, of a new human mind. Also, because society itself evolves, the interaction between any individual and his environment is subject to minor unpredictabilities. (Most elements of experience, to the soul, are fully predictable, hence my personal experiences of precognition — elements of my soul's forward projection into the future that somehow skip the normal blocking effect of the middle conscious and are exhibited in my conscious mind. Though these experiences are familiar to my base soul, my surface level mind has little ability to assimilate them.) Within your individual experience, however, most elements (and certainly all primary ones) of your experience are predictable. Your ambitions, dreams and achievements are the result of the interaction of the primary influences of your life. If you achieve a lot as well as aim for a lot, then you can be certain your soul, mind and corporeal body have united in some form of active harmony which can perhaps be best described as a point of human stasis.

Your goals in life, at least the primary ones, are implicitly the goals of your soul. Your surface level goals, such as that of owning a flashy sports car, may only be temporary infatuations of the mind, which are ultimately of little significance to the soul. Yet a goal to create or design a new kind of sports car is likely the goal of the soul, especially if you act on the desire seriously. (Many people have many passing fantasies of what they would like to do but are not really serious about doing anything about making the fantasy become reality — it's nice to just daydream.) Your life-goals are established by the soul. If you devote a major portion of your time and effort in pursuit of such a goal, your soul will provide elementary guidance and assistance. Usually this assistance is in providing your innate interests. Every interest you have is directly related to the goals of your soul. The natural biases of the soul shine through to the mind and though you may be taught to enjoy many things, the elemental pleasures of the soul will occupy your greatest efforts and, if possible, your indulgements.

The goals of your soul are not left only to your mind's devices, however. Some humans (indeed most) are engaged in concrete ways in improving the soul-race through improvements in human civilization. The soul effects these improvements by conceiving of some ideal it wishes to further or some element of learning it wishes to explore. By selecting a body and social circumstances that best lend themselves to the achievement of some aspect of that ideal (according, of course, to practical limits and realities), the soul embarks on the experiential course. In doing so, it must then use the body and mind to construct what it can of its idealized goals. If the effort is a failure, the soul has not properly prepared itself or has achieved little cooperation with other elements of society. Societal cooperation is the

Man's Imperfect Truth

key: few major endeavors may succeed without cooperation on the part of many souls and, very often, other living entities man has long called divinities.

These higher entities have long been associated with the human experience and have done much to cultivate human civilization. If they had not, human society would not have evolved so explosively nor so dynamically. In whatever context we conceive of these higher lifeforms, whether as gods or as good fairies, we can be certain that they have had a continuing influence on our lives. We have simply never come to understand that influence. Indeed, like the influences of the base soul, our minds seldom even recognize the influences of higher entities, choosing instead to assimilate that awareness as part of the physiological phenomena of life. It is only when something is interpreted as being purely external and *still* inexplicable do we turn to theories of the gods. The notions and theories of gods are universal to human experience. Every interpretation varies in content but not in essence. The notions we attach to such experience are often the result of overactive imaginations or miscontrued truths. The essential truth remains, however, that there are entities which are willing to assist the human world through individual human beings and evidence for this exists in these same embellished legends. Unless all the experiential accounts of such prophets as Jesus Christ, Mohammed and Buddha are discounted as superstitious hokum, there is little likelihood that anyone can deny the existence of some higher intelligently organized force which at times guides human endeavor. These entities, although they are not the named gods depicted in human religions, often present themselves as gods for the sake of influencing a given human being. More often, too, the entity is merely interpreted as being a god by the individual himself. Not having any other frame of reference to guide them during experiences of an other-worldly sort, people often interpret such an experience in a familiar, traditional religious sense.

The interaction with higher worlds is not restricted to religious leaders, though they provide some of the most famous examples. Indeed, most religious leaders became famous because of their concentrated dissemination of their experience and the willingness of others to follow where they led. Any human being may seek out such contact, though not all will be aware of having achieved it. For some, the contact just does not fit into their life-plan in a way they can be aware of in terms of their waking consciousness. They may not be intellectually prepared for such contact or may not be willing to undergo the study that sometimes must precede such contact. More, they may be inclined to reject any such plausibility simply because it interferes with their belief structure. Their weakness is not in their ability to perform the task of reaching beyond their own personalities through principles of the soul but to recognize the *possibility* of doing so.*

There can also be danger in making such contact, for many reasons. The contact may not be friendly or may be of a decidedly different philosophical bent (such happens, but rarely). The danger arises from the individual's reactions to the sudden induction into a world of awareness that he had heretofore regarded as beyond reach, even if he did accept that world's existence in intellectual terms. The truths he learns may be so intensely received that the individual cannot cope with them, the stress causing some mental disorder that disrupts his life. Also, the truths may be so contradictory to the individual's previously held value structure that he is forced to reevaluate everything he

---

*Many people, while stating their willingness to make such an approach to a higher world, really do not have their hearts in the effort. To be more precise, they set up barriers within themselves that both discourage the entities they are trying to reach and actually impair any communication that may ensue.

Man's Imperfect Truth

believes. That is a monumental task and is very dangerous in that too much old belief of value can be rejected in favor of misconstrued new truth. There can be social repercussions in terms of how friends and family react to changes that occur in the person (people sometimes turn away from friends when too quickly "born again"). Most of all, however, the danger arises from the individual trying to fully assimilate all the truths just learned. If told not to drink coffee or alcohol (as often happens during such communications), the individual may change his entire life pattern. It may improve his health but also cause other aggravations of physiology, some perhaps psychosomatic. The individual may take the new truths so seriously that he leads others astray, becoming the prophet of a new cult or sect (cults are merely the forerunners of religion, their acceptance and legitimization resulting from popularization). If that happens, and it often does, anything may follow. Christ's teachings resulted in the Christian movement systematically conquering the world. Recently, Jim Jones professed to have a divine inspiration to create a perfect society and led nearly 1000 people to a mass murder/suicide in the Guyana bush.

Although human society has many interpretations of the word god, the most useful is simply "entities of a higher nature than man which guide him". Most religions do not regard their divinities as perfect or supreme; they instead impart to them very human-like qualities mixed with their superior godly talents. The outcome of a relationship of a human being with such an entity is usually the attainment of some goal, the goal itself often set by the god. Without divine guidance, Hercules would not have achieved his 12 tasks, nor would David have slain Goliath. Yet without their gods, neither would have been faced with the tasks in the first place. Much of human history and myth concerns gods and at the same time violence. This violence indicates nothing more than the imperfection of any gods involved with us. Even the supposedly perfect Christian God decreed that "Thou shalt not kill", then proceeded to break that commandment Himself (according to the Old Testament) very regularly. Such failing may be regarded as godly imperfection, just as human failing is regarded as human nature. In the context of the gods' lives, as in human life, failure is a necessary part of the learning process.

From the perspective of the soul, the average failures of any incarnation are only the minute setbacks to be expected during a complex experimental process. For life is indeed an experiment, as is all nature. We merely get to direct to a certain extent elements of the experiment and try to control the outcome. Our goals, though grand when pictured in light of the common truth of Humanity, must eventually be distilled to the goals of individual human beings. Whatever cause or assistance those goals may represent, we must be certain we are the focal point of our own efforts. We are therefore primarily responsible for ourselves, though we may enlist the aid of vast powers, be they the powers of a collective portion of our own society or the higher powers of a god-like entity. Human goals, even though linked to the common goals of Humanity, must in themselves be the goals of the individuals who will attain them.

The average human being will die before he achieves all his life-goals. Because of the idealization of goals (as Jim Jones idealized the perfect society and tried to create it), failure to some degree is inevitable. Yet successes are relative. They are relative to both the past experience of the individual and to the experiences of those around the individual. Many humans, for instance, choose a business as a life-task. Their goal is to be successful in their respective lines of work and many are. Yet ultimately, the purpose of being successful, as related to humanity as a whole, will fail. The business, as a contribution to a perfect society, will not achieve the

Man's Imperfect Truth

human ideal. It may further the Human cause or, if the businessman worked to the detriment of his society through destructive self-interest, may actually hinder the cause. The measure of that individual's success or failure will only come following the life, when the greater awareness of the soul can be brought to bear in the evaluation of his various actions. Death is the great leveller of experience. It brings into focus the actions of a given incarnation, which is a chunk of the soul's experience. In the evaluation of that experience, mistakes can be corrected before they are too firmly implanted in the soul's awareness. Naturally, to enhance the soul's positive evolution, the in-flesh experience of the human being should be oriented to the ramifications of all actions. In other words, each human should understand as much as possible his "realm of effect".

When a human's life is over and the base soul and Spirit withdraw from the flesh to the Afterlife, the evaluation process begins. Naturally, there are things left undone, minor points which may not have had great bearings on the achievements of that soul. Yet there are many cases in which the soul for various reasons fails to achieve its primary goals. It may have set unrealistic goals or reached too high. It may also have found hindering circumstances too great for its will to overcome; or efforts applied may not have been enough. Seldom, however, is success judged in black and white terms. Between the polarities of perfect success and utter failure lies the vast range of partial successes. These partial successes are the guidelines for the soul's further efforts. Where successful, it may seek to apply greater effort to improve on that success during a future incarnation or it may regard its successes in that area sufficient and seek to shore up some area of weakness. And, given the vastly complex set of circumstances which involve each human life, the soul will undoubtedly see opportunities to both improve its successes and overcome its weaknesses. As it evolves into a more dynamic force, it will act with an increasing degree of efficiency, using strengths to overcome weaknesses and turning disadvantages to advantages.

The quest for success is part of the soul's need for self-improvement but the failures are largely disappointments of the mind. The mind, a much more temporal object than the soul, cannot afford to waste too much time in fruitless endeavor. Yet it is also the facet of experience least able to guide itself. It needs help, and because insufficient help (or guiding information) is available, the mind often fails to make good decisions. The soul itself has much more ability to analyze the circumstances of life and to abide by mistakes. Yet it, too, does not want to unnecessarily impede its development and will therefore do what it can to modify the human being's behavior (note that the term human being refers to that complex partnership of soul, mind and corporeal body). As the human being's personality is largely molded by the first two years of life, it provides a prescribed set of personality traits that will endure for that incarnation. The individual personality is the result of the combinative effects of the soul and corporeal body.

To understand the construction of personality from a union of body and soul, it is necessary to recognize the duality of evolution. First, life itself is the product of the soul, a separate process from the evolution of the corporeal body. Life merely inhabits bodies as they are required and evolves much faster than the bodies themselves. For example, humanity is currently the combination of a race of souls and a species of biological organism. The biological organism evolved over hundreds of millions of years (perhaps even billions) and has been elevated from simple protoplasmic-like matter to the very complex human form. In that process, the branching out of lifeforms has been tremendous, which means that the human being is probably directly related to every other biological lifeform on this plane. As evolutionary theory states, the human family tree can be traced backwards to show the various points at which major divisions began to occur. As described in Chapter 1, this evolution has survived as a biological memory in each organism, the memory being passed on through biological reproduction. Each individual organism adds its own minor changes to the overall history of change that is recorded in the biological structure. A single soul, on the other hand, need not be restricted by the slow, painful evolution of a vehicle. Because it evolves much more quickly, it uses a given type of vehicle for a number of incarnations, then moves on to a new, more advanced type of vehicle. The number of incarnations it uses any given type of vehicle depends on its evolutionary position: it may be a few lifetimes, a few dozen or even a few hundred. In time, a race of souls will evolve out of a given biological species altogether, leaving the biological species to another race of souls just attaining that level of evolution. In that manner, vastly new directions of evolution result for both the race of souls and the biological organism, a historical example being the evolutionary divergence of hominids from simians.

On individual terms, therefore, each human being is the product of both the long biological history of the human corporeal body and the exact life-experiences of the individual's soul. The body provides some impetus in the direction of the soul's evolution, for the soul cannot ignore the forces of environment which govern that body. Yet at the same time, the intelligence of the soul can motivate the body to do more than merely survive, as human history attests. It is that motivation that results in great progress in civilization; the actual changes in the biological organism in the same period of time are scarcely as significant. Humanity is aware of how much the human form has evolved over the past several thousands of years. It has become a larger, stronger (or at least healthier) form, mostly as the result of better nourishment and medical practices. Yet its evolution has advanced very little; most progress has instead been in terms of civilization. As any student of psychology can explain in detail, the human creature is not very far removed from his primitive roots. The "thin veneer of civilization" is easily stripped away in times of crisis, with a very animal nature surfacing, sometimes in horrible ways. For all the human struggle to master his animal nature, he cannot. The force of his biological history is too great; his soul is a motivator that cannot overwhelm the total reality of the in-flesh human being. Thus, the combination of a powerful soul with an equally powerful biological organism creates a curious combination of characteristics. There are the characteristics that indubitably belong to the body and those that indubitably belong to the soul. Together they shape a new force, the individual human being.

In that individual, there is a distinct personality formation. This personality evolves both as the result of the biological realities of the body and the experiential history of the soul. Although the soul's prior lives may have a great deal of influence in determining the individual's life-goals, they cannot entirely submerge the corporeal body's drive to reproduce or survive. The evolutionary ingraining of those characteristics is too great. Thus, the soul must learn to conform to those realities and use them to its own advantage. Naturally, this means the soul must to some degree "shape" its evolution in deference to the biological realities of the human body. In doing so, its efforts are governed in part by the body and subject therefore to whatever conflicts may result. The soul cannot achieve total success in its goals and has no complete ability to foretell every event that will occur within the context of a given body. But, with the experience of a number of lives in a given type of body, say a few human incarnations, the soul becomes quite adept at manipulating a basic corporeal form and controlling (or at least shaping) that body's motivations. Its instinctive ability to aid the physical mind produced by that body/soul combination will be greatly increased. Experience and familiarity, therefore, create wisdom.

Your wisdom, this inherent relationship between soul and body, is the governor of much of your human behavior. As a soul becomes more familiar with the mechanisms of the human body (every body, of course, has its own unique properties and talents), it is able to achieve higher goals. The aspirations of the mind, therefore, are only as effective as the base of experience which supports them. If the soul has relatively little experience in human flesh (say only one or two human incarnations), its highest aspirations may be far beyond practical grasp. In other words, the mind is a hopeful dreamer. Yet the highest goals may lead the soul to the greatest experience and any effort in that area will allow the soul to exceed its expectations of that life. An inexperienced soul may achieve more if it tries harder than an experienced soul with little ambition.

The physical relationship between soul and body also develops many of the actual personality characteristics of the individual. The soul, because of its many past incarnations (both in human flesh and the flesh of lower orders), has the greatest influence on personality. It, in essence, is personality incarnate, and also personality in formation. The actual life-experiences of each incarnation add to the soul, encouraging the soul to develop more or less of given traits. Yet the personality of a given incarnation, associated with a given in-flesh human being, is the merging of a particular soul with a particular body. Your personality emerges following the union of soul and flesh. The human body creates its natural impressions on the soul-matter of the base soul virtually immediately. As this joining occurs in the womb, the assumption may be safely made that the human in-flesh personality is already assured. Yet, as described in

Man's Unending Quest

Chapter 1, physiological circumstances that follow the joining may influence the personality. It is for that reason, therefore, that it takes until the second year of the incarnation for the personality to be relatively stable. This fact does not belie the reality that changes may occur later but these changes are usually elements of the maturation process, changes that occur because the mind itself gathers a certain amount of wisdom and control over its personality traits.

Your reaction to the events of your life as a mind depend on the body's physiological response to your soul. Because the mind is formed by this soul/body response, your decisions made during in-flesh life are largely predetermined. However, this is not to say that you have no freedom of will at all; mostly your efforts are the product of that long period of evolution that culminates in the unique point that is you. You are what you are because the influences in your history, both corporeal and soul, have made you that. Your mind is like a thin skin of ice over a large pond or reservoir that hides the collage of experience and past lives that lie there. Your prior lives were all as immediate to your consciousness at the time as this one is to you now; this one will recede from your presence as surely as the others already have. It will be added to the collage, expanding the reservoir that will become covered with some future skim of ice, a new mind. Your existence is continuous, nearly infinite. Your immediate presence at any given time is the "present", a notion that can only be defined as the instant at which you are aware. Any decision you make at that point is the virtually unavoidable result of all the decisions you have made in the past, many of which were made as the inevitable consequence of environmental factors. As your awareness floats forward in time, your decisions should become more managed by your mind and more in tune with the circumstances you seek to impose on your life and environment.

Man's Imperfect Truth

As you achieve various points in your life, you will find that certain elements of your experience impress you more than others do. The timing of these elements is not as important as your ability to recognize them. Most truths lie in waiting for individuals to discover them. Few are discovered as soon as they become available. Thus, you may be reading a book and a particular truth will strike you as exceptionally profound. As you underline it and attempt to commit it to memory, you proceed about your life, perhaps even applying that truth as much as you can. It is not, however, so much your sudden *knowledge* of a truth that caused the reaction as your *recognition* of the truth. The events of your life merely culminated at a point at which you recognized the significance of the phrase. Your consolidation of that phrase was immediate and very effective. Yet you may have encountered that same truth many times before and have never realized its importance. You may encounter it again and fail to see what so greatly sparked your interest. The key element of the moment was the mind becoming in active harmony with the latent knowledge of the soul. Most truths discovered in the atomical plane by in-flesh humans are known long before in the soul-world. In fact, many souls merely set about during in-flesh life to experience the things they have conceived of long before and try to make them happen as a real force that will add to humanity's progress. Their efforts are their life-goals and whatever success they achieve is a part of the experiential process of life.

When your incarnation is complete you then, as a soul, try to bring all the elements of that in-flesh experience in active harmony with the prior experiences of the soul. There is much that conflicts, for even in the Afterlife, knowledge and experience are interpreted subjectively. That is an unavoidable fact of life and any predetermined set of physical limitations will necessarily result in certain biases.

Yet the efforts of the base soul during in-flesh life are to guide these biases so that the individual achieves as much as possible. When there is great active harmony established between the human mind, soul and body, the greatest achievements are made. Naturally, these achievements are made only on the basis of the greater knowledge and experience of the soul. Mind, therefore, is not so much the partner to the soul as an infant brother.

Part of the goal of any incarnation is to gain greater control over the personality. It takes a great deal of effort and training to submerge personality traits yet the training can to some degree be effective. The essential point to understand in this is that although personality traits may be submerged, as we submerge to some degree the less pleasant aspects of our animal natures, we cannot eliminate them. They are simply rooted too deep, their core experience resting in the base soul, an area the mind cannot physically modify to any great extent during in-flesh life. If you don't believe your personality is basically established by age two and that its primary characteristics are rooted in the soul, try to remember the first time you experienced a major aspect of your personality, say grief or anger. If you think back to your first memories, you can probably recall that they center around some very prominent personality characteristic of that nature. You may also be aware that though you have encountered that same characteristic time and again since, your efforts to modify it have been either relatively unsuccessful or successful only to some degree because of great effort. You may recall, for example, a cherished pet being struck by a car or an event that made you very angry. Because the grief or anger suddenly swelled up inside you, does that mean it was born at that instant? Or does it mean the event merely released the characteristic, as subsequent events released the same characteristic again and again? Events of life merely trigger emotions or reactions. You then deal with those reactions as best suits your experience. If the event is new to you, your reaction may well be confusion. Yet rest assured that when you experience a similar situation in the future, you will be better armed to deal with it.

It is possible during in-flesh life to modify your reactions to situations but not to change your actual personality characteristics.* By reducing your anger each time a particularly aggravating situation recurs, you may gradually lessen the unpleasantness of having your anger control you. You instead control it. But control is not elimination and much of your effort is directed only to control, though you may consciously believe you are trying to eliminate it. Personality traits evolve only slowly, requiring many incarnations to create new ones or eliminate old ones. You may emphasize one trait over another but the actual change does not occur until the consolidation phase of the Afterlife. Your day-to-day life is a staging ground for experience, a filter for events and perceptions that will eventually be incorporated into the soul. As you approach the decisions of life with greater wisdom (both in terms of the soul and the mind), you may bring more

---

*Though a wound of the flesh or psychological impairment may change a person's behavior or surface personality, the soul is not usually hurt. The base personality remains unchanged. However, the wound or impairment may be such that the communications between soul, mind and body are disrupted to the point that the soul loses its moderating influence on the individual's behavior. Mental illness is often a case of physiological breakdown of the nervous system leaving the mind pretty much to its own devices. With the soul just along for the ride, so to speak, the mind lacks the natural guidance the base soul provides. The soul probably foresees the defect of the corporeal body before joining the flesh, or understands the conditions that will lead to some damaging accident. Yet it will take the risks inherent to such a situation for various reasons. For example, it may hope to overcome the weakness, learn from it or attempt to sidestep it. Also, it may have no choice other than to use an available vehicle, despite its shortcomings. Souls, when faced with the prospect of a greater duration in the Afterlife or joining a body that has an "accident" in store for it, will often choose the body. Natural disasters, car accidents and wars are just three causes of vast numbers of damaged and destroyed bodies. Obviously, the fewer there are of such disasters, the better it will be for all of us, in flesh and out.

positive changes to your circumstances than if you merely allowed life to take its course. You may find yourself able to get more happiness out of your marriage or encourage yourself to seek out a new career. As the new circumstances open new vistas of achievement for you, you actually remain the same. Your personality does not change but merely influences your life differently. Instead of anger or unhappiness being your controlling motivator, it is now contentment or cheerfulness. Your personality hasn't changed but your reaction to life's circumstances has.

Yet those changes in circumstance may have a profound effect on your evolutionary path. They pave the way for the actual changes that will occur in the Afterlife. As with the common psychoanalytic treatment of phobias, familiarity with life's situations eases painful change. In other words, if the lifestyle you choose is so characterized by unhappiness that it clouds everything you do, your discouragement and disappointment may become such an ingrained habit that the soul itself becomes unhappy and discouraged. That is the beginning of a disease of the soul and often the beginning of a disease of the mind in a future incarnation. Once the cycle is established, it is difficult to break. Thus, as psychoanalysts try to break phobias by gradually familiarizing the patient with the object feared, the fears of the soul can be broken similarly. In fact, often the phobias of the mind are phobias of the soul as well. The mind itself reacts to fears of the soul and events of an in-flesh life may trigger phobic responses and even strengthen them. Being clawed by a cat as a young child is not usually enough to instill a great fear of cats but if that same soul experienced say, a severe mauling by a lion in a prior incarnation and thus met a death, a very real fear may be triggered by that small housecat. The child's mind reacts to the fears of the soul (or its memory of fear) and seizes the event in a distorted manner. The fear of death, especially painful death, becomes

Man's Imperfect Truth

embodied in the archetype of a cat and all cats are feared.

Psychoanalysts would therefore seek to ease that burden of fear by slowly introducing the phobic individual to cats, first at a long distance, then over a period of weeks bringing the cat closer to the person until familiarization lessens or removes the fear. Because psychoanalysts do not often work from the perspective of past-life fears, they do not always reach this hidden depth and may not be able to solve the probem. There is, however, a budding effort in this area. One such psychoanalyst is Dr. Morris Netherton of Los Angeles, who wrote *Past Lives Therapy* (see reading list), a book describing his technique. In essence, he allows his patient to let critical memories of past lives surface to the conscious mind, then slowly familiarizes the patient with that experience. He has found his work to be effective in many cases and I can personally attest to the effectiveness of such a technique, as I have practiced a similar technique in past life recall (the results of which will be the subject of a future book). I do caution here, however, that past life recall can be a tremendous psychological phenomenon, stirring fears and guilts that you may not have even guessed you had. I do not recommend it as a parlor game or a technique to be used by anyone who doesn't wish to risk shattering his perception of himself and his world. As I described in Chapter 2, every human being has interpreted his conditions in a particular way and though undoubtedly is in some ways wrong, he is seldom willing to accept vast changes without some psychological trauma.

If, however, you do make vast efforts to improve yourself or your circumstances, you will find the efforts pay off when you undergo a similar effort in the Afterlife. Your familiarity with your mistakes and your failings will make them much easier to accept and deal with. You can discard over a period of incarnations many characteristics you consider undesirable. As you gradually lessen them as major forces in your personality, you can learn to manage them as part of your energy structure. As stated in Chapter 1, your soul is based on energy forms that are reshaped virtually at will to recall memories or to undertake analytical processes. The mind functions similarly and draws its core experience from life itself. It then adds this core experience to the soul during consolidation. If the soul chooses, it may direct certain experiences to the forefront of consolidation activity and these experiences become the catalytic sources of energy for the consolidation process. Thus, certain experiences can be virtually "burned out" of existence, though the usual procedure is merely to lessen them. The actual burning out (or devolving into waste heat) of any experience is risky: that experience could lead to many more significant experiences in the future, if properly managed. Thus, an undesirable trait, such as anger, can be turned to a useful tool of self-preservation — all tales of the Incredible Hulk aside, the human body can and does have physiological reactions on the basis of anger that can stimulate a greater strength than normally provoked by mental command. Other undesirable traits, be they a tendency towards laziness or some other virtually innocuous reality of existence, can be brought under control and perhaps even put to good use. In this sense, therefore, the soul may occasionally indulge in a little lethargy to renew its sense of devotion or interest in a given task.

Self-renewal is one of the major tasks of life. There is, of course, the physiological renewal of the corporeal body and soul undertaken by the intake of food energy (or sunlight, heat or other energy), but in addition to this there are other forms of renewal. One in-flesh humans are familiar with is psychological renewal. We are all familiar with the state of being somewhat jaded, or tired of a given task. The task becomes a burdensome chore instead of a source of fun or enjoyment or learning. Just as the human mind can

Man's Imperfect Truth

become bored with a task, so can the soul. Its task may span many incarnations and may therefore become somewhat arduous and many parts of it redundant. It can get bored with learning the same basic experiences over and over, yet it should always seek to improve or in some way modify those experiences. Like the mind, however, it sometimes becomes too lazy to do so and this laziness may become a factor in its future evolution, an actual impediment to progress. The soul may become like a jaded teacher, facing rows of bright-faced children year after year but teaching them the same material. For the children, the material seems new and enlivening. For the teacher, motivation becomes a tool to be struggled with and great effort must be made to maintain the enthusiasm the children deserve.

The mind and soul upon separation from the flesh are much like bottled water that is frozen and the bottle broken away. The ice retains the shape and impressions of the body but is free to return to its liquid state as circumstance permits. The soul and mind in the Afterlife, therefore, are like the frozen water trying to retain its definition in the face of heat or weathering. Unlike water being refrozen in a similar bottle, however, the same soul/mind combination cannot recapture the experience of the flesh. The base soul and mind, joined in an active harmony, gradually relinquish the specific characteristics impressed upon them by the realities of one body and define themselves according to the natural principles of the Afterlife. In so doing, the memories of the past life are retained, as are the memories of every other life. The new merely gets woven into the fabric of the old and predetermined processes construct a new definition of purpose. In that manner, the soul, as a constructive entity, defines its future and adds to its past. Its present, therefore, is the momentary analysis of the Afterlife, a complete fusion of mind and base soul into the new cohesive entity, the Soul.

Your identification with a mind is not as absolute as

your in-flesh life would have you believe. The attention and precedence we give as in-flesh entities to the cares and woes of this world often matter for little in the Afterlife. What perfume we wear and what color our clothes are have little more relevance than the passing sensory pleasures they provide. Yet who we spend our lives with and what we do for a living are very important to the soul, for experiences such as this provide the basis for future evolution. If they are constructive, future evolution may be more constructive still. If destructive, however, the future is in peril and evolution may well be impaired. It is easy in our world to become so wrapped up in selecting pretty baubles and trinkets to adorn the body that your energy is distracted from more worthy pursuits. Yet these practices may also be a valuable tool of relaxation, the need for art and sensory pleasure an element bringing much happiness into a life that can create a more positive atmosphere for progressive evolution. Contrary to the old Calvinistic theories in Protestantism, progress need not be bought through denial of the flesh. Pleasure and work must simply be balanced forces, working in active harmony. Most of all, if your life's work brings you your greatest pleasure, joy can be your paramount characteristic.

Harmony is one of the soul's greatest tasks. If harmony can be established, evolution is fostered. The greater the harmony, both of self and of society, the greater can be unimpeded evolution. Thus, there are extensive Karmic practices in any soul-world which delineate individual behavior. Elements of this Karmic Courtesy are practiced in our world as the conventions of polite society. These conventions grow up around the practicalities of in-flesh life, such as eating or meeting another individual, and are related to societal habits more than any absolute guideline. The only absolute that exists between all reasonably advanced living entities is that there must be some codified behavior that

Man's Imperfect Truth

guides interaction for mutual benefit. Thus, it may be good manners to belch after a meal in some countries but bad manners to do so in North America. The conventions themselves mean little, but the social requirement for such conventions is great. Thus, the circumstances of the in-flesh world very much affect the direction of the soul's evolution; it determines the type of experiences that may be gathered and also to a large extent how the soul can react to those experiences. Further modification of the soul itself is necessarily made within that context and the Karmic conventions of its life must be bent to fit the mold.

Thus, the human body is more than a useful vehicle for the soul's evolution. It is also a guideline, through its very existence and use, to what the soul may become. If the soul does not apply itself vigorously to overcoming some of the traits characterized by the animal nature of the corporeal body, then it may be a long time in achieving the higher world it desires. It must therefore discover its own way to the higher world, working out its problems in unique ways to pave the way for the essential changes in self it requires. It must also be careful that it does not develop new traits that will impede its progress and must find a way to correct its past mistakes. In essence, then, though the human creature does have a soul that guides its actions and this soul is often aided by higher intelligences who reside in the worlds the soul seeks to join, its future is not totally under control. Environment plays a major factor in shaping experience and though the soul can predict such major calamities as earthquakes and hurricanes, it cannot avoid them entirely. Some victims will be claimed; it is up to the Karmic conventions of the Afterlife to decide who will use those bodies. In such a circumstance, a soul may wish to atone for a past error and take a body that will be harmed by the calamity; it may even be left such a body by lack of choice. As in-flesh humans, our minds can only skim the surface of this reservoir of knowledge and try as hard as possible to make the right choices. No matter how much of our earthly existence we come to understand, we will never be fully able to outguess the plans of our base souls. Though in some ways we may perceive ourselves as being victimized by the process, we are also, and probably more so, helped by that life plan. Our understanding is necessarily limited by our direct evolution of mind from body and soul; we must therefore accept that we are a part of an awareness we cannot fully explain or control. We can only continue to function within that awareness and do the best we can. That is our truth.

4

THE WHOLE TRUTH vs. PARTIAL TRUTH

There is Truth and there is truth, the difference being that Truth is perfect and truth merely truthful, or fragments of some perfect Truth. As discussed in Chapter 2, man will know no perfect truth, even though he may define perfect laws. Thus, he may define a paradigm which accounts for much of the universe, perhaps even exploring much of reality according to mathematical principles, but he will never define the complete universe. For in defining absolute laws, he must then relate them to himself, a process that can never be complete as long as he evolves and changes. His definitions of reality are based solely on his perceptions and his perceptions are entirely captive within his incomplete perspective of a far greater force. Though he knows that many of the laws and principles he discovers are mathematically precise and hence perfect, he can never be certain that he knows all there is to know of a given law or how it interacts with all other laws, known and unknown.

Ultimately, there is only one Truth in the universe and that is the understanding of the universe and all in it. This understanding is achieved only in the context of the entire universe for no element of it has the complete perspective necessary to define everything in it. Thus, man would come to know the full Truth only if he were the universe itself; as a fragment of it, his perspective is limited and hence so is his understanding. Even his own reality, however he chooses to define it, remains a partial truth for he is ultimately only a lesser part of a greater whole. If he could evolve as a separate, self-contained entity, the human being could then aspire to perfect knowledge, but only of himself. His understanding of any other totally separate reality would be blocked by the fact that he would have no awareness of or connection to it. If such an awareness or connection existed, he could become in some way a part of it or a partner with it in some greater whole. Thus, man's truth is a partial truth and his efforts, though aimed at uncovering the greatest Truth of all, are doomed to fail. He may only define greater and greater truths, extend his search to an ever-greater paradigm of existence. As he uncovers more and more laws, transcribes them into the perfect relationships of mathematics and assimilates this knowledge in a manner immediate to him, he will evolve a greater knowledge of self, a greater truth.

Man is in search of truth. Even his efforts to survive are the formative influences of his quest for truth, his learning to survive more efficiently and more comfortably driving him onwards in his quest for greater truths. Man seeks to improve himself through his quest and has found satisfaction in many elements of it. As he learns, his hunger for knowledge grows. He learns to survive better than before and uses his experience as a springboard to even greater knowledge. He has steadily progressed in knowledge throughout history. This improvement is the result of each individual human being's efforts to better himself and his society.

All human beings have an innate desire to better themselves. This desire may manifest itself in peculiar or harmful ways but is always there. Making things better for the self doesn't necessarily mean making things better for anyone else but a healthy individual always strives to better

The Whole Truth vs. Partial Truth

his society as well. Naturally, individuals don't always agree on *how* society is to be improved. The result is pretty much what you see about you: many individual humans interacting in society as they each see fit. Many make great efforts to unify the individuals into a harmonious whole and their efforts are to some degree successful. Overall, humans live in ordered societies that only occasionally fall into utter chaos, such as sometimes happens during wars and natural disasters. Such destruction is not random. To the soul, much of it is fully predictable. But at the same time, the soul knows it cannot always avoid it and must pay the price. This feeds the anger and frustration that often boils in human societies. Far from there being a structured plan laid carefully out by some all-knowing divinity as some religions suggest, life happens for the most part as it appears on the surface. The actions of souls guiding the flesh meld themselves into the overall efforts of the in-flesh being. The result is various cultures and societies functioning according to conventions and mores developed over many, many generations.

The human being's behavior depends on three factors. First, the characteristics and history of the base soul. Second, the characteristics and history of the corporeal body. And third, the characteristics that emerge when soul and body are joined. Together, these characteristics form a personality within living flesh. The flesh is then directed to perform certain tasks according to the base soul's original desires and the desires that emerge with the formation of the new personality. This new personality may be very similar or dissimilar to the personality that emerged in any prior incarnation. The continuity is the experience brought forward from each life in flesh. The variables in a given incarnation are therefore determined by a particular soul joining a particular body and the environmental and social circumstances to be encountered in that incarnation. Considered in total, the vastly rich experiences encountered in any lifetime are really mostly predetermined by established conditions. Once the base soul decides its preferred course and chooses a body, a set of principles are established which that soul is committed to. The body will live in a particular environment and society and will have certain biological skills and certain limitations or disabilities. Most important, there will be a defined set of people it will primarily interact with, that is, a family and close friends.

These interactions of each individual with himself and those around him form the society as a whole. Societal structure evolves from the efforts of individuals and the traditions and practices they accept and employ. Societies are evolving things, based on all experience of any fore-running societies that may have influenced them. Nothing about any society is constant. Everything in it evolves, just as the individual soul evolves and the corporeal species evolves. This evolution can be measured and categorically assessed in terms of various scales, each scale the subjective tool of the assessor. In other words, if you seek to measure the collective scale of intelligence of a given society, you must establish an intelligence scale by which to measure it. In the Western world, the Intelligence Quotient scale is used with some limited success in this regard. Its main fault as a tool lies in its structured tests which are inevitably biased for and against particular portions of a given society. Although we have not devised the ideal tool for measuring intelligence, the IQ test does provide a rough gauge of measuring one individual against other individuals. In any measurement task, it is the concept of relativity that enables the measurement to take place. Distance is divided into hypothetical points based on the units of an arbitrary scale. Consistency of fact, therefore, is based on the consistency and accuracy by which the scale is applied. Precision is achieved in relative terms to what has been achieved before.

Souls have constructed an elaborate concept of

The Whole Truth vs. Partial Truth

measurement based on stasis. Each point, or level, of stasis, to the soul, is a definable point in an evolutionary progression. Because everything evolves (that is, changes continually in some way), everything must be measured in relative terms. The selection of measurement scales is therefore based on definable points in that change. These points may be of two sorts: the first is physical points in which something happens within the entity being measured to identify the point it has achieved, such as a baby learning to walk; the second is an arbitrary scale divided into consistent portions, such as a yardstick. The first type of scale is determined by the nature of the entity, resulting from the physical forces that affect its evolution. The second is constructed as a tool of convenience, largely for the purposes of communication between individuals. Both types of measurement scale are necessary to assess reality. Because one of the fundamental functions of the soul is to assess reality, the measurement scales used by souls reflect both their physical experience and their conceptual experience.

Souls divide aspects of stasis into three main camps: physical stasis, biological stasis and stasis of soul. Each of these main divisions contains many specific measurement scales which souls actively apply in assessing reality. The number of scales is not constant because they are potentially infinite; a scale can be devised to measure anything. In-flesh life is a curious combination of the three main categories. Each facet of an individual's life can be measured in terms of the physical nature of the material comprising the individual, the nature of the biological organism and the evolved characteristics of the base soul. Each of these areas defines aspects of the individual as a means of assessing those aspects in relation to other individuals and aspects of physical nature.

In defining any system such as the human being, it is necessary to dissect the system in many conceptual ways.

Man's Unending Quest

Each part of the system is therefore considered separately from the system as a whole so as to understand the whole system better. This, in science, is called "reductionism". The opposite concept is "holism", or the study of the system as a whole. The soul is adept at both methods. Although the only truly complete whole is the universe, many parts of the universe can be contemplated as systems. Each system, therefore, has some form of fundamental unity which provides a basis for separating it conceptually from other systems. In identifying and measuring these systems, souls have evolved the concepts of stasis. Each concept of stasis reduces some facet of existence to terms which can be analyzed, rationalized and assimilated. Most of all, shared concepts of stasis allow the results of this analysis to be shared. Each point of measurement is a point of stasis and can be conceptualized and communicated.

Physical stasis, as used in soul communications, is the active harmony of matter. It defines the nature of matter for purposes of conceptualization but does so according to the nature of the matter itself. Thus, an atom has physical stasis because it exists in a state of equilibrium as an atom. If the atom is converted to another form of energy (atoms are, in a sense, "frozen" energy), it loses its stasis as an atom and gains a new form (or forms) of stasis in whatever type of energy (or energies) is produced. Also, as smaller systems within the atom, the proton has stasis in its existence as a proton, the electron as an electron, and so on. Such unity of form is never permanent and consequently stasis is never permanent. It is merely a temporary phase of physical stability within a defined context. In that same sense, the planet Earth has a physical stasis because it exists over a period of time in essentially the same form. Changes occur within it, but the stasis lies in its overall, large-scale equilibrium as a system. On a larger scale still, the cosmos has a definible stasis, even if still expanding as quantum

The Whole Truth vs. Partial Truth

mechanics suggests.

Quantum mechanics also suggests the ultimate form of stasis. To souls, this stasis is Supreme Stasis, the point at which all matter in the universe is reduced to a common physical base. Physicists call this state the Big Crunch, the implosion of all matter to an infinitely small base. It opposes the Big Bang, which they theorize was the beginning of the universe. The Big Crunch, to some physicists, is the end of the universe. Quantum models can provide little guidance for what lies beyond, except another Big Bang. Souls, whose powers of assimilation of physical forces are much more highly developed than that of in-flesh humans, basically agree, but see the reduction of matter to a common base as being an infinitely broad field, rather than an implosion. Whatever the end result, it won't be a permanent state. The common wisdom of the soul indicates that if any state were ever permanent, the universe would not now be evolving (i.e., changing). Therefore, it is highly unlikely that any state to be encountered in the future is permanent. If the Big Crunch comes, therefore, it will be a point of physical balance and inherently unstable, just like everything that occurred before has proved ultimately to be unstable. The Big Crunch would therefore come and go, passing like every other moment. Time at that point will not likely be relevant. As Einstein pointed out, time is very much relative to the physical matter that perceives it. If all matter is completely uniform, then time itself must at that point be uniform. It would not progress during the Big Crunch, but be a timeless instant that would occur and pass, over as soon as it started. A new universal incarnation would then erupt in a Big Bang and be similar to or different than whatever universal incarnations came before. The universe would go on its immortal way, shaping worlds, defining and changing matter (or something else, as the case may be) and evolving towards the next Big Crunch/Big Bang. And once again, it would start all over.

Although the number of universal incarnations may have already been infinite and there may be an infinite number more to come, the number of incarnations of any soul using human flesh has not been infinite. There have been a distinct number of incarnations that each soul has experienced and each fling in the flesh adds one more. For any given human soul, the number may be one human lifetime or hundreds. It all depends on the history of that individual. The fact that a group, called a race, of souls is using human flesh is only a matter of convenience. This race of souls has adapted itself to using one species of corporeal body. Any race of souls is limited to using one biological species or a few closely related biological species because of the physical natures of both the soul and the body. In short, they must be compatible. Although souls can and do periodically join new corporeal forms, the progression evolves over a period of time and through specific patterns of incarnations. Certain points of biological stasis and stasis of soul must be compatible. Both these forms of stasis depend on the forms of physical stasis associated with each soul and each species. In our world, the biological species are constructed of atomical matter. A soul evolved to use these biological forms can join certain individual bodies within the species according to more specific criteria. On the other hand, a soul evolved to use the astral energies of another plane for *its* incarnations cannot use the animal bodies of this plane at all. That is why our guides appear so rarely in this world, except as ghostly apparitions.* Their entire matter structure is different from our corporeal bodies, even though there are great similarities between the

---

*Our guides can also appear to us within our minds as telepathic images. This often happens during dreams and crises when the biological body is not the focus of consciousness. Raymond Moody points out that many people who die and are revived see spiritual entities while out of the flesh (see *Life After Life*, reading list).

The Whole Truth vs. Partial Truth

matter of their souls and ours. These similarities of soul characteristics enable us to interrelate in certain contexts but not so far as to share the same biological organisms as evolutionary vehicles.

To illustrate this point, consider the evolution of man. At some point, there was a vast change in the nature of this species from an ape-like or simian construction to a man-like or hominid construction. That change occurred over millions of years, the last radical twist being the evolution from Neanderthalis to Modern Man. This last change in evolutionary direction was relatively sudden and like other equally wrenching changes before it was the result of a new race of souls taking over the corporeal species as its evolutionary vehicle. The prior race, which had in turn taken over from some still previous race, moved on to another level of experience, likely a higher plane of existence. There, those souls undoubtedly continue their evolution using some new vehicle, while our race of souls continues to use the human species. To use this form, our soul race had to evolve certain characteristics over a long, tedious period of time. They did so on this plane using the lower animal forms (I will describe the actual evolutionary schema in a future book). Before even that, the souls of what we now call the Human race had evolved on what are called the "lower planes", where very simple and basic lifeforms come into existence, their origin based in simple "near-life" constructions. With this primitive history behind us (our souls did not, of course, all originate at the same time, but over a period of time), the current race gradually came to cohere into a unified group of souls.

This group of souls now has a set of characteristics which define them as a race which is a fundamental form of stasis of soul. This grouping is based on the physical characteristics of the soul-matter which constitutes each soul of the race. There are closely related races with much the same characteristics but are just sufficiently different to warrant a different taxonomic grouping. (They also use different biological vehicles.) Man has constructed a taxonomic chart of the biological species in an analogous fashion. When soul races are closely related, they use closely related corporeal forms. If there was another species of Man, our race of souls would be able to use that species too, just as the same souls can use any of the biological races of man. Closely related races of soul use the other higher primate species as evolutionary vehicles and less closely related races use the other species of mammals on a descending scale. Other classes of biological animal have less closely related races of soul still. The taxonomic associations, therefore, give each race of soul a group of functional vehicles to use in much the same way that biological species eke out their own ecological niches. The success of any race of souls in relation to its vehicle depends on how well adapted the soul is to the body. Once again, the measurement of this success can be observed, determined and predicted according to the various types of stasis achieved by each primary element of the system, the living organism.

Biological stasis relates to specific points in an evolutionary scale of a biological organism or species. A human being has achieved a stasis in biological terms that sets him above all the other animals of this world. We can devise various scales to measure particular aspects of this stasis but all boil down to the simple facts of man's achievements. He has done more than any other animal, therefore his point of stasis is higher. This statement is, of course, over-simplified but essentially accurate. In like manner, a beaver has achieved a higher point of biological stasis than a wasp, though both construct elaborate homes for themselves. The wasp functions more on the basis of genetic programming and less on the basis of intelligence. Given adequate tools of measurement, the differences

The Whole Truth vs. Partial Truth

between man, beaver and wasp can be applied to various scales and quantified. Such a reductionist technique would verify the holistic assessment that man has indeed achieved a higher point of biological stasis.

Another form of biological stasis is the relationship between individuals within a species. Again, scales of measurement can be applied. A human baby develops certain motor skills in a more or less sequential manner. In learning to walk, the baby generally first learns to roll over, sit up, crawl, then stand. Each achievement in this scale is a higher point of biological stasis. The skills learned by a human being are levels of achievement that vary in many terms and, because the human being is a system which includes a soul, cannot be fully separated from the motivations of the individual which are rooted in the soul.

As the soul evolves, it achieves certain capabilities that it applies in in-flesh life, usually in the form of motivation. These capabilities are related to the exact material construction of the soul, or the soul's own physical stasis. The soul is constructed from a particular material and has a physical stasis on a holistic level: its individual existence. This form of stasis is equivalent to the physical stasis of an atom. Its greatest difference, of course, is that the soul lives. However, just as the atom cannot sidestep its material reality, the soul can't either. The soul can only change itself over a long period of time and, at the human level, does so through the medium of the human corporeal body. Having evolved to a point at which they are compatible with the human body, the souls of this race require that vehicle for their further evolution. The physical stasis of our race of souls requires that each human soul join human bodies for in-flesh incarnations. Each incarnation then changes the physical nature of the soul to a minute degree, ever-so-slightly elevating that soul's point of physical stasis. This cyclical pattern of reincarnation is common to many lifeforms on many planes. It is a means of converting nonliving matter into living matter, a means of growth for the individual soul.

Souls are therefore responsible for their own well-being and growth. A soul will not allow itself to "devolve", or deteriorate in terms of its physical stasis. Before this happens, the soul will always join another body. Thus, the Second Law of Thermodynamics applies only to nonliving matter. An atom may eventually lose its organized state as an atom and enter less organized states, but lifeforms will always become more organized and more complex. Evolution of life, therefore, is progressive, not regressive. Once a lifeform begins to evolve, it continues to evolve.

Within a given universal incarnation (the period between the Big Bang and the Big Crunch), life cannot become non-life. There is no death in the sense that life stops; there is only the death of a living organism, such as the human corporeal body, when the actual life-force leaves it. Life, in that case, has not ceased. It has merely moved to a different locale, leaving rubbish behind. Because of these principles, there is a cumulative effect to life. Once life is established, it produces more life for itself. If it evolves to a great enough level (or achieves a certain point of stasis, to phrase it differently), a lifeform can conceivably create new lifeforms. By this, I mean a different sort of creation of life than biological birth. Biological birth merely uses existing vehicles to create other vehicles under the guidance of already-living entities. A genuine creation of a new lifeform is to manufacture the stuff of life, to cause simple energies to converge in ways that construct new energies called "near-life" energies. These near-life energies may be likened to the nearly organic materials science now assumes existed in the so-called "primordial soup" of early earth. Near-life is close to being life but is not yet independently alive. Certain entities more advanced than man can manip-

The Whole Truth vs. Partial Truth

ulate energies in this way, just as we already manipulate chemicals to create nearly organic substances (scientists do this by running electricity through basic elements such as carbon, hydrogen and oxygen in a water solution).

After creating near-life, the next step is to elevate the energy structure to the next major level in the chain of physical stasis: to life. To be life, there must be some elementary form of consciousness that will eventually be capable of self-direction. Defining life is a difficult task, perhaps even impossible. Although the definition I offer here may well be imperfect, there is no doubt that there is somewhere a division between living and nonliving matter. The soul itself assimilates this difference on a holistic level at all times, though it takes a relatively advanced form of soul to study the division in reductionist terms. Man, as a soul-based lifeform, is approaching that level of ability. Man's guides, whom he often calls gods, have already reached that point and have tampered with the basic stuff of life. In fact, man's religions and myths, specifically the Creation myths, indicate that man's guides (or gods, if you prefer) have had a direct hand in creating the individual life-forces that have evolved into human souls. This creation was not, of course, an instantaneous thing, but a long process that continues at least in terms of their guidance and probably even continues with the creation of new souls who may someday join our race.

As human souls evolve, they motivate in-flesh humans to study the elements of existence to build an understanding of their origin. Souls in their discarnate state as a general rule know far more about the origin of humanity than in-flesh humans do. Yet this knowledge is not easily translated from the holistic knowledge of the soul to the reductionist knowledge of the human mind. This book is one primitive effort in that regard; perhaps my techniques can be refined. At this point, however, I am certain that the efforts of man are closely observed and supervised by other entities who have had a major role in the origin of each of us. These entities are not the creators of the universe but, like us, are a part of the whole. They are simply more advanced. As they guide us to greater truths, we come closer to mirroring the tasks they have achieved themselves. Perhaps someday man will create life out of nonliving matter as they have.

Still, the ability to create life does not explain the origin of the first life. This, I am sure, is the result of the natural elements of the universe acting in perfectly normal and naturally controlled ways (that is, by physical laws). These forces that create life are sister forces to those that create non-life, such as atoms. If an atom, a complex structure of matter, can be created more or less accidentally, so can the more complex structures of life. As an evolving intelligence, the human race has only its own curiosity to spur it on in its quest and only the ingenuity of in-flesh humans to actually build empirical experiments. Without our corporeal bodies, we have very little ability to shape matter. This is not because soul-matter cannot shape atomical matter, but because human souls are not as skilled at this as they might someday be and other entities already are. Thus, we know the human life-force can move a pendulum and there have been reports of objects as large as tables being moved through psychokinesis. To do this usually requires more accident than design on our part. We have simply not learned to develop and exploit skills that are usually just seeds within us, our psychokinetic abilities often surprising us more than acting under our control. Poltergeists are therefore sometimes real effects caused by unrecognized powers within us (and at other times the poltergeist really is a disruptive discarnate soul). Mind over matter, as such effects are often called, can provide healing effects for our bodies or cause ulcers. It is all in how well the ability is used and how much of it there is to use.

The Whole Truth vs. Partial Truth

Although Western science urges us to stay away from concepts such as psychokinesis, this is more because science is unable to deal with the concept in reductionist terms than because of its physical nature. The efforts of the base soul or mind to manipulate matter directly rather than through the medium of the corporeal body are often uncertain and unpredictable. Recreating any such efforts in a laboratory setting is at least equally uncertain. Coupled with the lack of a model of any supposed physical nature which would allow widespread study of such phenomena, the study of psychokinesis and other extrasensory effects is crippled. However, there are so many *natural* facets of our nonsensory (or, in other words, non-corporeal) existence that science does both itself and humanity a disservice by avoiding the area. Scientists fear being tainted with the word supernatural, when what they are really avoiding is experience of the non-atomical. In fact, thought is a non-atomical effect of the soul (coupled with the mind) and scientists would be as far ahead to reject thought as being impossible as to reject psychokinesis, telepathy, clairvoyance or precognition.

To perceive something as complex as the human being holistically, it is necessary to study the environment as well as the subject. After all, the material entity is definitely the product of the environment. Yet this environment is vastly more complex than any modern-day scientist conceives. It is far more extensive than the atomical universe that we perceive with our eyes and telescopes, extends to far more minute areas than we sketch with our computers and electron microscopes. Our survival as a human species is not assured by our relative permanence as soul-entities but by our need for the human form. If we could acquire or produce a better vehicle, we would do so. In fact, part of the soul's efforts when in flesh is to improve the physical stock of the species. Medical science, social programs and the development of physical abilities through sports are all efforts guided by the soul. The human body, generally speaking, has become larger and healthier through the ages and perhaps even stronger. If we would only let go of the distrust and conflict that mires so much of the world in war and despair, every human society could be as healthy as any in the Western world. To aid his limited body, man has developed a myriad of machines and tools to exploit even the most hostile environments of this world. We have expanded civilization to the coldest Arctic regions and the hottest tropical zones; we have begun to harvest the potentials of the oceans and the skies. Space may even become a frontier of colonization. All this effort is directed at building safe and habitable environments for the nurturing of corporeal bodies (and the experiences to be gathered using them) for the use of the soul.

Corporeal bodies are essential to the evolution of the soul. The vehicle determines the type of experiences a soul will have and therefore the course of evolution that the soul must follow. The soul attempts to direct the corporeal evolution and succeeds to some limited extent. Overall, however, the vehicle does establish the limitations for what a soul can achieve in a given period of time. Man, to experience the principles of flight, must go to great lengths to construct machines to fly. For centuries, man tried to create machines to fly but succeeded only recently. The human experience of flight, despite our machines, remains limited. The human soul, on the other hand, when independent of the corporeal body can and does fly. It can experience the freedom of movement this accords but does so by sacrificing its ability to manipulate its physical environment the way in-flesh humans can. The determining factor in limiting experiences when incarnate or discarnate is the environment: the atomical environment of this plane establishes a set of limitations and the astral environment of the Afterlife establishes a different set of limitations. In

The Whole Truth vs. Partial Truth

the cyclical pattern of reincarnation, the soul must abide by each set of limitations in turn, doing what it can all the while to improve its situation. This improvement is slow, arduous and often painful. But it is evolution.

Earth, as an evolutionary vehicle, is far larger than meets the human eye. The cohesive bonding of the planet is founded in its atomical structure (hence the atomical plane is often called by souls the "base plane"). Within the limited range of bonding properties of the atoms is a set of less restricted planes (less restricted because they do not respond directly to the force of gravity). These planes have bonding principles of their own which are not dissimilar to the bonding properties of the soul itself. A human soul is therefore subject to many of the principles of these other planes, regardless of its "presence" in the atomical plane (i.e., when joined with atomical flesh). These other planes exist on a physical spectrum of matter, based in higher frequencies than our usual devices can measure. Radios, televisions and even our eyes are receiving devices for various frequencies (or more specifically, bands of frequencies). Unless a device is designed to receive a given frequency, it does not receive it. Thus, you do not catch television signals as a normal rule with your AM radio. But if something goes awry, as often does, you may be surprised at the results. There have been reports of people receiving radio signals on their braces; an analogous situation is when a human being sees a soul from another plane. These crossovers of effect are startling for us and spark our tales and legends of ghosts and apparitions. But they do happen and occasionally happen because a soul wants to be seen in this world. When a person dies, a loved one may be informed by an apparition of the dying person. Such apparitions are not the usual experience but occur often enough to be generally known.

These other planes exist on higher frequencies than

atomical matter and are often the cause of extrasensory perceptions. Psychics refer to them as "vibrations", an inexact term that is strangely expressive and therefore popular. The planes, including the atomical plane, are held apart from one another by physical laws, perhaps analogous to two magnets holding each other apart when like charges are opposed. The barriers between planes are certainly not impossible to cross and the apparitions I have just discussed are an example of such an event. A more disciplined example is the crossing over of souls from this plane to our Afterlife. The Afterlife is joined with our world in a peculiar arrangement that differs from the relationship between our plane and that of, say, our guides. When we die, our souls cross over into the Afterlife, slipping through a barrier that is normally closed to our conscious minds. Likewise, when the soul joins a fetus, it crosses this same barrier, going the other way. The soul slips through this barrier by configuring itself in a sympathetic manner to the energy barrier. Just as a neutrino can slip through atomical mass causing hardly a ripple, the soul can arrange its own transport through a normally incompatible field. Recall the magnets with like charges opposed. If the magnets could rearrange their polarity at will, one could easily reverse its polarity and they would then leap together instead of push each other apart. The soul can rearrange certain elements of its being to achieve many goals. One is the crossing over of energy barriers that normally restrict it and another is to remember images of past experience. This remembering is exactly the same process you use virtually every moment. As you may well imagine, the soul becomes quite adept at the skill over time.

We maintain our in-flesh perspective because it suits our immediate purpose. For most of us, remembering our past lives or our time in the Afterlife is not crucial. What is crucial is the gathering of experience to further our

The Whole Truth vs. Partial Truth

immediate and long-term goals. That is why the mind can forge ahead along its sometimes lonely path. The soul is there guiding it, as are other souls of the Afterlife and our special guides. Yet the mind does not need to be consciously (in our everyday, waking sense) aware of this guidance. It can, of course, be useful to understand the nature of this guidance because experiences can then be optimized according to the skills and abilities of the individual. But it is the skills and the abilities of the individual which ultimately define success.

The human soul does not need the human corporeal form per se; it does, however, require a form that provides this level of skill if it is to advance to a higher level of skill. If our soul race did not use this form, another would take our place. Nor will we relinquish our vehicle to another race before we are ready. As individual souls move on to join a higher race, the majority of souls of this race will continue to use the human form. Eventually, some other vehicle on a higher plane will be in a suitable position for us to move on *en masse* to take up a new direction in evolution. At that point, another race of souls will take over the human form and the biological species will undergo changes not seen since the dying days of Neanderthalis.

Because of the integrated structure of many planes within the planet Earth, the human environment is vastly more complex than we can possibly realize. Though we may casually think of the immediate biosphere as our environment, our evolutionary processes are governed by incredibly vast ranges of reality. The gravity of atomical earth, for instance, shapes our bodies daily. Over generations the stooped, ape-like formation has been gradually replaced by the confident, erect form we now enjoy. The gravity of other solar bodies also has subtle effects on us that we seldom note. The moon pulls the ocean tides: at the same time, it influences human behavior through the biological medium of the human body which is 70 percent water. Even distant stars affect our lives directly, an influence the often denigrated field of astrology endeavors to define. Though astrology as a science is only as effective as the skills of the people using it, we do not even have an infant science studying the effects of other planes on our behavior. These planes are as much sewn into the fabric of the universe as the atomical plane we study so carefully. By ignoring the soul and its extensive environment, we are ignoring vast reaches of our external and internal experience.

As man comes to understand more of the forces which govern his life, he can improve his existence and his ability to generate worthwhile experiences. Naturally, his efforts will be defined largely by his environment, the experiences determined by what is happening according to the natural laws of the universe. If the movements of tectonic plates cause an earthquake, some people are bound to be hurt. The soul cannot change the fact that the plates shift. It can only join a body which is remote from the danger zone or motivate the in-flesh organism to move away. It may, if it is inclined, organize its own evolution around the prediction of earthquakes, perhaps joining a body capable of developing the skills of a geologist. If it does so, then it has accepted a "life-task". Essentially, each of us when in the Afterlife conceives of a life-task and attempts to implement it during in-flesh life. The complexity or difficulty or even importance of the task depends on the desires of the soul; success in achieving the task is dependent on the skills of the soul in guiding the in-flesh organism.

The major effort of the soul when in flesh is to direct the organism to fulfill a purpose. Once that purpose is fulfilled, the soul may remove itself from the body. It may also remove itself from the body if the effort seems to be a failure. At that point, an "accident" may occur, enabling the soul to leave the body. Death is usually predictable to the soul. Because the soul can "read" the characteristics

The Whole Truth vs. Partial Truth

of a body and the physical circumstances it will find itself in during the incarnation, it can project what will happen. It may see failure or success but will probably plan its life around the inevitable. If the chosen fetus is deficient in some critical way, the soul is able to pinpoint the exact point the organism will die. It will determine when, where and how major influences occur and strive to build success into the incarnation given those constraints. While in flesh, the soul will provide a manipulative form of guidance through desires and motivations. Most of the goals of the incarnation will stem directly from the soul.

For any large-scale success, the soul must forge an effective harmony with the mind. The mind begins to form the moment the soul joins the fetus. The conditions of that mind, like those of the body, are inherently predictable to the soul. The soul will therefore have a strong sense of how much success it will achieve in that incarnation before it starts. Even though the soul accepts the shortcomings of an available situation, it may not always be able to achieve enough harmony of action with the other elements of the incarnation to be successful in a given task. In other words, the efforts of soul, mind and body may not be in active harmony, or in an agreeable state of stasis. Many forms of self-conflict may result from such a situation and psychiatrists become familiar with many of them. The conflict may be especially traumatic when a soul is ill-prepared to join the flesh after a poorly conducted consolidation phase. If these internal conflicts can be resolved during the in-flesh life, many of the symptoms of psychosomatic problems disappear. In fact, the efforts of a soul may simply be to resolve problems it has in adjusting to its place in its environment; just as people can be unhappy, souls can be unhappy. In fact, most unhappy people are unhappy *because* their souls are unhappy. Problems in in-flesh life are usually just the symptoms of greater problems of the soul. If efforts are made to resolve these problems in the flesh, the effort required to resolve the problem in the Afterlife will be lessened considerably.

The experiences of in-flesh life have a great impact on the soul's evolution. Unhappy events such as wars and natural disasters do much to interrupt the evolution of the soul. When battling for survival, the in-flesh organism rarely has an opportunity to develop an enlightened, casual approach to life. The soul, therefore, must make do with the experiences it is forced to accept and may do so in a mature, responsible manner, or not. It depends entirely on the individual and that individual's history. As human beings struggle with the realities of this world, the soul must accept its limited ability to affect the outcome of its efforts. Ultimately, the soul must learn to foster cooperative evolution and leave bitterness and hate behind. Not all souls are now able to do this, as the hate and bitterness in our world so gruesomely demonstrate.

Each event in life is the culmination of a long series of causes. The soul in guiding the organism can only try to interact with these events as best as possible. To some extent, this means fighting the baser desires that motivate the organism to take the easy way out. A weak soul does not always succeed in driving the organism along the "high road". That is why there is violence, rape and arson. That is why there is insanity and war, hate and greed. The best desires of the soul may not be enough to guide the individual and, worse yet, the soul may be at fault. If there is such a thing as evil, it is in the malicious intent of one soul to gain at the expense of others. In the end, such efforts are counterproductive. However, the wayward soul does not always realize this, or if realizing, does not care. On the positive side, these wayward souls eventually correct their behavior. This correction does not occur until they have caused much harm, and other souls follow in the wayward footsteps. Because of Karmic laws of cause and effect, bad things cause more bad things and therefore harm can spread like fire. The safeguard against this spreading of harm is the efforts of each individual to act in the best interests of everyone, because good causes more good. Eventually, we must hope, man will put his entire house in order and all of us can live without threat of war and unprovoked violence.

Once imbedded in society, however, any influence dies out slowly. There is a training process of one in-flesh generation to another that ensures corporeal attitudes change slowly, despite the attitude of the base soul. Only vast amounts of effort and relearning can redirect the attitudes of an in-flesh society. Consequently, most souls accept rather than fight the direction the society will force them to follow during in-flesh life and adapt to it. They may even carry these attitudes from one incarnation to the next, further imbedding them in the psyche of the people.

Our susceptibility to misconceptions of truth as in-flesh entities stems from the relative lack of knowledge that each newborn mind has. Although the soul carries with it a wealth of experience and wisdom from one life to the next, the mind is a new creation with each incarnation. It has no previous experience of its own. Consequently, it develops both according to its natural tendencies (supplied by the soul) and the teachings of its society. The mind's knowledge of self develops during one incarnation and ends when that incarnation is over. It is then literally absorbed into the base soul. While in flesh, though, the base soul is submerged within the biological organism, the control of that organism resting in whatever mechanisms stimulate the nervous system to action. In this regard, the mind has the upper hand over the soul because the mind is close to being the only controlling intelligence over the nervous system. Other intelligences may indeed act upon the nervous system, but not without interacting with the mind at the same time. Thus, the patterns of knowledge and conceptualization established in the newly formed mind during childhood are usually dominant for the duration of the incarnation. Though the soul can motivate the mind to test and perhaps change certain beliefs, its control is not absolute.

As teachers are fond of saying, young minds are like blank slates. These blank slates are easily filled with all sorts of conceptions and misconceptions but not entirely independently of the experience and knowledge of the base soul. Also, the corporeal body does provide indisputable evidence of perception which also affects belief. If something is proved wrong by the perceptions of the corporeal body, the mind is not likely to accept it. When perception is coupled with the strength of wisdom of the soul, the mind can be effectively guided in determination of truth. Where it is not so readily guided is in terms of man's spiritual beliefs. Most spiritual beliefs deal with matters not readily apparent to corporeal senses. In determining spiritual truth, the organism's greatest tool for testing truth is virtually useless. In fact, the corporeal senses are often counterproductive in terms of defining spiritual truth because crafty teachers can easily mislead the innocent on the basis of fabricated perceptual "evidence".

Santa Claus, for instance, is a delightful myth that is foisted onto most children in the West. Trusting children believe their parents because they have faith in the people who cherish and nurture them. Then, Christmas morning, the perceptual evidence is there: presents under the tree and a stocking filled to overflowing. Any hidden doubts about the plausibility of a single old man flying about the world in a sled drawn by reindeer is erased: until, of course, time reveals the deceit. At that point, the parents may try to salvage their child's faith by telling him of Santa Claus as the "spirit of Christmas", a less than satisfactory alternative

The Whole Truth vs. Partial Truth

for the saddened child. In the same religion, the modern interpretation of God as an ill-defined "spirit" is the product of that exact same process. Gone is the idea (for most of us) that God is like a wise old man; instead, God is a concept, an undefined force which we seek but don't really care to define.

The natural wisdom of the human being is guided by the soul and is responsible for that individual being able to correct many of the delusions that are created by the developing mind. The mind is just a conscious awareness soaking up experience like a blotter. It tries to assimilate all that experience into an identifiable paradigm so that it may encounter facets of its reality repeatedly without making the same mistakes over and over. Its training process allows it to learn to control a body, which it uses to gather further experience. As the individual becomes more experienced and more motivated, the mind can direct the body to perform more and more specialized tasks. This process is essentially the same cyclical configuration as every other facet of living evolution. Life always begins as a very simple, basic awareness that gradually builds to more complex levels of experience. The motivation to perform higher tasks comes with the evolution of ability to do higher tasks. Once established, this cycle drives the entity to ever greater achievements. Thus, an individual who learns to do something inevitably learns to do it better if he practices. He learns to walk, talk and control as much as possible his biological functions. If he practices a certain natural skill to a degree, he may use it to improve his experience in that body tremendously. Yet these skills and motivations are seldom apparent at a young age. Our principle physical skills develop over the first dozen years; mental skills develop over the first twenty. Though personality is established by age two, the abilities of that individual will be produced over a long training period. This training period ultimately lasts the entire incarnation, though many individuals allow their pursuits in life to wither.

The formative process of the mind teaches the youngster much about survival. Thus, the children in a playground are exercising their skills. They are running and jumping, developing their muscles and coordination. Seldom will you see them practicing on a voluntary basis the conceptualization of freedom, love or human dignity, though they often project these qualities in their behavior. Their behavior is usually an acting out of what they are, the expression of their dreams and emotions and interests, a development of mind and body in preparation for a life-task. This life-task will take them years to complete if it is complex. If it is not, they may pursue it for years anyway, gaining many useful experiences from the mere fact of being in flesh. In each life, they practice skills, arts and relating with other living beings. The lifetime training period adds much to the overall goals of the soul and many experiences are repeated over and over to strengthen and improve them. The soul has a natural stake in each in-flesh incarnation to learn from it as much as possible. Though the new mind learns much during the formative years of childhood, to the soul these years are largely redundant experiences from many childhoods. Thus, the soul wishes the incarnation to survive to adulthood to carry out its plans and to explore and rationalize its ideas. Only then may constructive resolutions to life's prior experiences occur. It is therefore to the soul's advantage to survive in the flesh for as long as possible, to glean from it every possible experience.

Thus, the ultimate harmony of mankind and environment is absolutely necessary to provide the soul with the most positive learning experience. The soul cannot fully guide the mind at any point in the in-flesh incarnation but is least able to do so during childhood when the mind itself hasn't fully developed its skills. The interface between mind,

The Whole Truth vs. Partial Truth

body and base soul requires the practice of experience before it functions efficiently and relatively faultlessly. The child is more susceptible to natural disasters than the older person because of inexperience. As the child grows to biological maturity, it should also mature in its goals and personal efforts. Ultimately, all of us should work towards universal harmony and accord. Wars cause needless destruction and though they provide valuable learning experiences, equivalent experience can be achieved in less destructive arenas.

The pursuit of knowledge for improved health or environmental conditions also helps the human organism to survive longer. All the facets of our society are geared to helping our biological organisms survive longer so that the soul may make more use of each body: much time is lost during the reflective period of the Afterlife when no suitable body is immediately available. More time is lost when the new body is being trained. To enhance human survival, therefore, is to enhance the evolutionary potential of the species. More, the better the quality of the experience, the greater the learning opportunities gained. Modern technological society, as a collection of skilled technicians, offers more learning experience than the subsistence lifestyles of undeveloped regions. Hence, the development of the world vastly increases its evolutionary potential.

Although developing the world is an important task, it is possible to threaten that very world while doing so. The technical advances that make life so rich in the industrialized world also threaten to cripple that world through nuclear war, pollution and the unplanned rape of our resources. We are a careless and greedy species and need to temper these traits with organized development of all our societies. Granted, there is a short-term cost involved which governments, corporations and over-taxed individuals don't care to carry, but the alternative is worse. We often speak high words about leaving a better world for our children. Perhaps we would be spurred to greater care still if we realized that when our souls reincarnate, those children will be us. Our own self-interest is vested in developing the greatest truth we can.

5

THE CREATOR

All life has its creator. Not all life, however, was specifically created by the Creator. One, creator, is a concept of Truth. The other, Creator, a concept of Truth. The usage of capitalization, as defined in Chapter 1, denotes completeness. A truth is merely a unified part of Truth, thus incomplete. Its unity does, however, allow it a functional identity which remains dependent on the whole: it only appears to act independently. Conversely, Truth is complete, a perfect and all-inclusive totality. Any force, therefore, which creates such Truth must itself be perfect and all-inclusive and therefore synonomous with the truth it creates. By that definition, there can be only one Creator, a perfect entity represented by all that exists. This Creator is synonomous with the universe, which is the physical reality of all that exists. To souls, the Creator is the creator of the universe.

However, to say the Creator created the universe and then say the Creator *is* the universe does not explain the origin of either. There is a mystery even among souls as to how the universe originally got rolling. Although some physicists consider the Big Bang to be the beginning of the universe and the Big Crunch to be the end of it, souls see these events as only turning points in universal evolution. To the soul, the universe is an evolving entity which lives and dies in a cyclical sense. Yet it never ends. Thus, souls can use their powerful deductive abilities to "see" the origin of this cycle of the universe, the most recent "Big Bang". They can also "see" the next "Big Crunch". But despite this cosmic sleuthing, they remain unable to see into infinity. The real nature of Creation remains beyond the soul's power to define.

Still, the belief of souls at the human level is that there will come a point at which each soul is evolved enough to know and understand how the universe came to be. They hold this belief because they have been instructed by higher entities which in turn have been taught in much the same way by higher entities still. The chain of teaching is perhaps as never-ending as the universe itself but all life eventually comes to hold some curiosity about the universe's origins. One of the principle notions that derives from that curiosity is that of the Creator. It is debatable whether one should think of the Creator as a living being or a nonliving being. It is certain that at this point the Creator cannot exist as a living being as fully expansive as the universe itself because the universe at this point is not fully alive: it is only partially alive because it contains matter which is not alive. The Creator, therefore, is an idea that souls share but have little hope of experiencing directly.

Because man's guides have strived to teach him of the Creator in some elementary way, many human cultures have developed Creation myths. In fact, most of these myths were evolved by primitive peoples who used their intuitive abilities much more readily than modern Western-educated peoples. These myths portray the Creator as a powerful spiritual entity which established the universe and then created humans. Genesis provides our most familiar Creation myth, but the Creation myths of many other peoples are strikingly similar. Often, because the peoples who originated the myths were primitive, they confused the entities which were

The Creator

teaching them, our guides, with the Creator. Thus, in Genesis the Creator becomes synonomous with the specific guides of individual human beings in later Biblical stories. It is perhaps disturbing for the devout Christian to think that the concept of divinity that he holds is a case of mistaken identity, but that is often the case. The Creator spoken of in the first brief paragraphs of Genesis is the originator of the universe. That Creator does not exist *in that form* any more, even though some Christians still believe so. There is now a universe made up of living and nonliving energies that always change and do so according to universal Laws of Nature.

Our guides, however, have long tried to bring us closer to understanding our origins. These origins do not necessarily have to be considered in the same breath as we consider the origin of the universe because as lifeforms we have not been around that long. But now that we are here, we can certainly try to learn *how* we got here. We can do this by delving more deeply into the concepts of both creation and Creation.

Creation, with a capital, is all of the universe as created by the Creator. A creation, on the other hand, is only something new. One concept is the bringing into being of *everything* that exists from *nothing* and the other concept is the bringing into being of *something new* from the stuff that already exists. Likewise, the Creator brought everything into being from nothing and creators merely bring into being something new. Small "c" creators, therefore, are really only arrangers. By that definition, of course, even humans are creators. Although the chances of fulfilling our hopes of uniting with a universal Creator are remote indeed, we can still be happily assured of our ability to rearrange matter. One of the most remarkable things we can do is to create living matter from nonliving matter. Though we do not create new lifeforms (we do not create new souls, only new soul-matter), there are entities who can. Certain of our highest guides can create new lifeforms and probably do so all the time. How they do this is beyond our current ability to know but we can be certain we will someday advance far enough to find out.

The creation of new lifeforms is a goal of man, though we have so far failed to even adequately grasp what life is. We can create nearly organic substances from base elements but cannot imbue them with life. We express this creative urge in our reconstruction of lifeforms and other material realities that already exist. In doing so, we have shaped life enough to introduce new species to the world. A mule, for example, is more than just a subspecies altered through genetic variation. It is a cross between two species, creating something new to the world.

Human notions of creation vary. We have certain elemental understandings of the creative processes of the universe but have hardly begun to explore them. Consciously, we are very limited animals, even though we are less limited than our lesser animal brethren. Although our minds allow us to function as conscious entities, they do not always allow us the access to the soul we should have to pursue our interests to the greatest possible degree. The mind does not show us how we came to evolve, though the soul could; instead, the mind hides behind the corporeal senses and builds a wall of awareness around itself to protect its own fragile existence. Although man has discovered great truths, these truths are subject to the interpretations of the mind. Thus, the truths are severely limited. If we consider a concept of a day, for instance, we usually interpret it as we see the day we are currently experiencing, a somewhat arbitrary definition of 24 hours of darkness and light that has vastly different connotations from one part of the world to another and from one season to another. We usually forget or don't bother to consider the fact that other planets

The Creator

have days which vary even more. If we think of the universe, we tend to define it only as what we can perceive, not the vast reaches beyond even imagination. We hesitate to open our minds to vast unknowns because we are afraid to. Though we often do not realize the source of this fear, the soul sparks some of it because it knows too great a revelation of truth can destroy the mind. As in-flesh entities, we are therefore partially blind without knowing just how blind we are. We cannot easily stretch our minds to encompass ideas that are not directly related to experience, such as the fact that it is equally logical that the universe should be endless and that it should have a beginning and an end.

Human souls have a common base of philosophy that finds its way into earthly religions and philosophies in varying degrees. This is the Karmic Way of the souls, a method of living based on their philosophical precepts. These precepts are the highest that human souls have been able to develop and build into their living existence. The efforts of the souls to conform to these ideals often result in the personal efforts of many in-flesh individuals to inspire or contruct new ideals and to develop existing ideals. We can see evidence of the souls' Karmic Way in our need to believe in higher direction and in the overall structured evolution of the universe. Humans exhibited this need long before there were scientists to explore the universe as a material reality. This embryonic need stirs in every human heart and whether it is ignored or nurtured depends only on how well that individual is in harmony with the Karmic Way. Every human society evolves its own common philosophy or way of life, its own Way, that provides members with a set of ideals for existence and societal expression. Whether that expression is through Communism, Catholicism or something else, the human need is to believe in greater harmony and system and to have faith in these guiding forces. Although human philosophical beliefs have many differences, they also have similarities which indicate a common base of human experience. The differences only mean that no philosophy has achieved a harmonious totality that can be described as Truth.

The Creator is not a passing notion. The concept is dictated by the existing state of affairs in the universe. Like a gap in a scientific paradigm, other known facts point to it. The missing piece needs to be explained. That we fail to explain the missing piece does not mean we have to reject the premise. We only have to try harder. Our greatest fault is that we confuse the origin of the universe and material reality with the origin of ourselves. In trying to understand and explain one, we try to reach the other too directly. Just as our many myths of Creation point directly to the past and link the Creation with the beginning of human experience, or the beginning of a given tribe of humans, our scientific paradigms are still missing many elements in the equation. Man did not leap into being in an instant; nor did the universe as we know it leap into being in an instant. There is an evolution in both man's history and the history of the universe and it is this evolution that we must detail. The origin of the universe was a long, long time ago, the result of forces we will never fully understand. As it came into being, it started a long chain of events which eventually resulted in this particular incarnation of the universe, part of which is the planet Earth. Through further evolutionary process, this planet came to contain human life. When primitive peoples came to rationalize the origins of themselves and their universe, they could not possibly be expected to understand enough to spell out the history of universal evolution in detail. Thus, very generalized statements of Creation came into being with very localized contexts. Though it was perhaps a natural impulse that caused many human cultures to regard themselves as the focal point of Creation, such belief cannot possibly be

The Creator

expected to hold true in a greater analysis, such as is possible with modern scientific tools. Each of these primitive societies evolved the best belief systems they could in their circumstances. There is no reason to assume, however, that the greatest truth spelled out by any such society is a complete Truth or will remain the greatest truth that the society will ever devise. The Bible, for example, was the greatest truth of the people who wrote it. Even though modern scientific knowledge has surpassed the knowledge of physics of that day, modern societies have yet to live up to certain of the spiritual truths taught in the Bible.

Man enters truth as a bather enters the ocean. The little he can truly understand is the little the bather sees. His perceptions are lost in the opaque distance, limited by his need for oxygen and his ability to traverse the waves. The greatest truth lays beyond him in the unseen depths of the ocean. He sees only a few shallow feet. That is the human lot, to see only a small bit of this vast and wonderful universe, but we may indeed see more and more of it through our efforts as a well-equipped diver may learn more of the ocean. To open further knowledge to our grasp, we need only consolidate our purposes.

Our understanding of human purpose is naturally related to our understanding of our material being. What are we? How did we come to be? These questions have plagued humanity for many millenia and will plague him throughout his future. That he will never understand the full nature of his origins is as simple as the basic fact that he cannot learn the ultimate origins of the universe. Yet he can learn the specific details of human evolution, the evolution of a corporeal body and the evolution of the human soul. Though we cannot learn the perfect equation of the universe, we can and do learn more equations and perfect many of the imperfect equations we have already come to know or suspect. As long as the human mind is

Man's Unending Quest

housed in a limited shell such as the human body, perfect Truth remains a very distant goal, though the questing mind should never be discouraged. Questions unasked never receive even imperfect answers.

Our intelligence is the foundation of our quest. There are many other species in our world which learn intelligently, including the higher species of mammals. Yet humans learn far more than they do, orienting the quest for knowledge to greater amusements and use. We are the only species on this plane which learns (and teaches) for learning's sake. Though our learning process stems from our animal need to survive, we have evolved higher purposes. Our higher purposes and our animal natures often conflict, making us the often oblivious victims of two separate realities. Our material needs conflict with our spiritual needs, providing us with a source of growth and of disaster. We have many higher ideals which we pursue with vigor, at all times subjecting them to the lesser but equally motivating ideals of survival. Thus, we have medical research and war; police officers and muggers.

In human history, there has been a natural tendency to equate the word "material" with facets of bodily survival or pecuniary wealth, such wealth merely being a convenience that translates into various stages of individual well-being. The word "spiritual", on the other hand, is generally related to aspects of higher endeavor or motivations that transcend mere corporeal survival or well-being. As a species, humanity has become extremely wealthy, wealthy to the point where the problems of the world could easily be solved if trillion-dollar military budgets were redirected. Not every problem would be eliminated but every individual human being on this earth would be given vastly greater opportunities for spiritual advancement — the ability to learn for learning's sake. With the needs of immediate survival oriented to a spiritual quest for knowledge at the same time, even the

The Creator

world's poorest societies could elevate themselves to widespread efforts in improving the human species, as members of Western societies are now reasonably able to do. Yet the spiritual impoverishment of the world (disregarding the many, many fine efforts made by individuals) has forced the world's material wealth to languish and rot. Humanity has not yet gathered the wisdom or motivation to alleviate its full extent of poverty.

We cannot spend our way out of poverty because we have not yet achieved inter-societal accord. If we could achieve this accord, our vast wealth could be geared to alleviating all forms of human suffering, suffering which continues only because the human animal hasn't the general strength of will to redirect the course of his evolution. Much of this unwillingness is the fault of the governments of the world's various powers: they cannot trust each other to drop their arms and pursue total harmony. Sometimes it is higher ideals which interfere, each proponent of some major philosophy trying to foist it on his neighbors. At other times, it is simple human greed and lust for power. Most of the time, it is a combination of these forces, outgrowths of the human animal's need to find a better way to survive and to extend his realm of reference. Our nature is oriented to the defense of the self, therefore we have vast military budgets when we join in vast societies. The perceived threats are often real threats, as one untrusting neighbor is all too likely to attack another equally untrusting neighbor, or power-hungry ideologues unhesitatingly attack those who won't bend to the ideology. Simple unilateral lowering of arms, as some naive masses of demonstrators in Europe have recently demanded, would be disastrous. A disarmed enemy is an all-too-tempting target. We are, in essence, trapped by our own nature, the victims of a reality created by our own evolution. We can only hope to gradually bend our future evolution to a more palatable nature, creating for ourselves less destructive realities.

Because we were not simply created as perfect entities which somehow failed to continue to be perfect, as Christian mythology suggests, we have very real problems to solve. These problems are resolved only on the basis of in-flesh experimentation, on the Karmic basis that every living entity must correct its own faults. Just as the natural biological processes of evolution cause a species to adapt to environmental conditions, an intellectually oriented species such as humanity must resolve the special problems it faces during intellectual advancement. Other entities (our guides) are willing to assist, especially if assistance will in some way improve their own existences. Overall, however, humanity's problems belong to humanity and humanity must be the primary motivating force in solving them. Many of these other entities have influenced human history, guiding individual humans on the basis of their greater experience. These humans, through Karmic ripple effects, have taught other humans much. Vast power structures can thereby come into being to push a particular type of learning. Christians build organized churches, Communists commit acts of violent revolution and democrats promote democracy. Every set of ideals exhibits some of the facets of Truth. All have failings and shortcomings — all are only the imperfect constructs of a living experiment.

Because we have experienced help and guidance from other living intelligences, our philosophies, mythologies and belief systems incorporate these realities. Our religions mythologize the teachings of higher entities in ways the original human contact could assimilate them. Thus, the shepherd who has a vision of the origin of the universe interprets it in light of his own experience, a very small world indeed. If told of higher worlds, the images he creates in his mind are naturally referenced to what he understands his world to be. Modern man is not excluded from this

The Creator

individual interpretation. Undoubtedly the "city of gold" envisioned by early Christians was similar to the cities of the day, modest collections of mud-brick homes. The more modern inclination would be to see a city of golden highrises. If we envision these higher entities, we may see their bodies as being shaped as ours are, or they may even present to our minds images of themselves that are distinctly human-like. For all we know, they may even be shaped as we think they are but chances are they aren't. We have only modelled their world in our image, made the forces of higher life intelligible to ourselves by translating their concepts into our own. With the abilities of these higher intelligences to shape our lives, we can be certain that to the unsophisticated human mind that they seem very remarkable and god-like indeed. Whatever they ultimately prove to be, we can be certain that no entity man has known is the Creator. Our gods are only creators, like us, even if they are much more creative.

Our spiritual knowledge does not necessarily conflict at all times with our material knowledge. We have divided the concepts intellectually for our peace of mind and our quest for discovery. Because we analyze our environment sequentially, dividing material reality into packets of unity that are intellectually manageable, we do the same for less material concepts. The truly spiritual is pure knowledge; the truly material is physical reality. Both are ultimately one and the same, viewed from different perspectives. One, knowledge, is the understanding of the universe, or Truth, and the other, physical reality, is whatever forces comprise that universe or Truth. Understanding, of course, can only come with life and thus can be said to be a facet of life. Conceivably there could be material reality without spiritual reality. But because there is life, spirituality does exist. When understanding begins to evolve, we can be certain the spiritual forces of the universe have begun to manifest themselves. As humans, we struggle to understand our material reality; our spiritual truths for the most part lie just out of our collective grasp. Yet we can be certain that the ultimate goal of all lifeforms, however distant in likeness to humans, are attempting to define the Truth of the universe. That is life's task.

If there came into being a unified consciousness that encompassed the entire universe, creating the all-knowing Truth that true spiritualism holds as its ultimate goal, we can be certain that it would be a holistic moment of awareness. It would not last, for it would somehow break apart into the fragments that allowed it to achieve that harmony. The ultimate intelligence would be like the nonintelligent "Big Bang" of physical theory. It would tear itself apart into the creative aspects of itself, creating again a new incarnation of a nonliving universe in which life and intelligence would evolve. When that life again achieved a supreme state of stasis, it would again break apart and begin yet another universal incarnation. Whether the human intellect decides in favor of a living or nonliving origin for *this* incarnation of the universe can only be based on an analysis of this incarnation's history. How far back we can trace this universal incarnation, however, remains to be seen. How far are humans willing to extend their imaginations?

The truths revealed through expanding our imaginations are only indications of what we can eventually find if we sift through material reality long enough. To do this, we must stop fearing imagination and calling the products of human imagination false without benefit of careful analysis. Human imagination is only the recombination of familiar events and knowledge, and therefore contains much truth. We have only to describe to ourselves the truest elements as opposed to the less likely. In that manner, much of human mythology can be melded into a universal paradigm. Our perceptions while in flesh are weak. We don't see what the

The Creator

soul sees, or even realize what it has seen in the past. Our holistic interpretations are based on sequential analysis, which means that our frames of reference are always inadequate. We cannot and have not analyzed in a sequential and rational manner all that the human being has holistically perceived. Essentially, we are faced with a dilemma: do we believe the inadequate paradigms created by the sequential analysis of science or do we believe the holistic perceptions of the soul? Neither perception is adequate for our minds to be fully at ease in the modern world. Somehow these two forces must marry into a cohesive entity which will allow us to explore the unknown in a manner compatible with our techniques of sequential analysis.

In terms of humanity's origins, we have knowledge both from scientific investigation and philosophical (or religious) tradition. The two seem to have inordinate conflictions but we should realize there is not an uncloseable gap between them. What isn't provable by science today will either be eventually proved or isn't worth retaining anyway. For instance, the conflict between Christian Creationists and Darwinists is totally unnecessary. The Creationists don't seem willing to accept the evidence before their eyes which proves the human being has evolved from ape-like ancestors. The theory, they say, contradicts their preferred notion that the universe and all in it was created in seven days (counting the day of rest) in the year 4004 B.C. Yet their belief is based only on a calculation of geneological notes in the Bible and a very vague chapter or two in Genesis. On that slim basis, they choose to reject very valid archeological and geological data and theory. In fact, they stoop to no end of philosophical cheating to support an obviously fallacious argument. Some Creationists publicly claim, for instance, that man could not possibly have evolved from horses and dogs. Yet the theory of evolution says no such thing. Uninformed or unsophisticated people may fall for this emotionalist trickery and that is its only danger. Man, evolutionary theory states, is the evolutionary product of a history of corporeal influences that began at a very simple biological level and culminated some hundreds of millions of years later in the human being. In the direct chain of evolution linking man to these simple lifeforms, there are many definable phases or steps in an otherwise unbroken continuum. Man, horses and dogs may well have evolved from common ancestors very long ago, but they are in no way evolved from each other. As man long ago diverged away from his closest relatives, the apes, the indication is that he will continue to evolve further apart from them in the biological chain.

The unwillingness of some people to release themselves from untrue notions is an obvious result of indoctrination. They have been taught to believe a certain thing and cannot let it go, even if it is proved wrong. Yet many beliefs never really die; they merely get transformed and worked in with other beliefs. Furthermore, some of the beliefs held in religions that science currently looks askance at will eventually be proved to be correct. The brief truth told in Genesis of the Creation is valid, if considered in light of physics. This particular belief is mirrored so many times in other mythologies that science should be pulling together the commonalities to measure them against its own reasoning of universal origins. Thus, instead of allowing the Genesis Creation myth to fuse with the origins of the Judaic peoples as the history is related (a chronological series of events, to be sure, but not one that was effected in seven earth days), it should be considered in light of modern knowledge. As discussed earlier, this incarnation of the universe may well have been the result of a diffusion of a universal consciousness that evolved into what the universe is now. Or, it may be that primitive peoples have personified the natural nonliving forces which erupted into the Big Bang,

The Creator

giving these forces a humanized personality which was later projected onto the beings who guided Abraham, Moses, Jesus Christ and the other prophets of the Bible. The very specific history of the Christian-Judaic tradition may well include some reference to the ultimate Creation. Naturally, the account is very generalized and provided in only a few sentences. The bulk of the verbal history is the legends and accounts of a given tribe of people — longer and more detailed because the people were able to relate better to events closer to them.

The historical confusion of the Creationist could well stem from the concept of seven earth days as opposed to seven days in some allegorical or numerological sense. Numerology plays a major role in the Bible and numbers such as 3, 6, 9 and 12 sprinkled throughout the Bible have many meanings to souls. The number 7, especially, has great numerological significance beyond its context as seven earth days — to souls, 7 means love.

Though the exact meaning or original interpretation of the truths offered in the Bible or any other religious text may always remain beyond our grasp, blind obedience to any dogma is futile. There is no way the wishes of a few sentimental folk will change the absolute nature of the universe just because they wish to disagree with scientific discovery. Many diehard notions people associate with their religious truth are hard to substantiate even in the light of the source text. An idea that once served a useful purpose (not necessarily a purpose of promoting accurate knowledge) may be retained through forces of societal inertia long after it becomes relatively useless. Christianity, Judaism and Islam have evolved out of common traditions, branching out from the source just as evolving lifeforms branch away from common ancestors. As time passed, new truths were added in local areas and new prophets came to individual peoples. Thus, whole societies have emerged with vastly different ideas than their common ancestors, melding truths and rituals of many cultural experiences into new and varied ways of life. Yet something always remains of the earlier teachings and common traits continue to surface again and again under the guidance of human spiritual nature.

Science experiences the same evolutionary trend. As it becomes a greater and greater force, it fragments itself into various courses and paths which explore certain avenues more closely than others. Though each course ignores to some extent all other courses, the actual separation of disciplines is an illusion. If we choose to explain the total universe in terms of atomical theory, then we must ignore anything that does not fit into atomical theory. Many modern scientists do just that. Their experience is self-limiting. Not wanting to disrupt their comfortable view of existence, they ignore anything that will disturb it. Conversely, some scientists may wish to prove some cherished view or theory and will go to great lengths to bend or falsify data to support it: though this isn't the scientific ideal, scientists are human beings and subject to the vanities all of us are. If the theory is that the human consciousness cannot survive outside the human flesh, then no amount of evidence, experiential, circumstantial or empirical, will be enough for someone determined not to be convinced. Nothing short of surviving bodily death itself would be convincing enough. The reluctance of many Westerners to believe in life-after-death is exactly this tendency: it is contrary to preferred theory and people are reluctant to consider evidence that will force them to change their thinking. It is easier to ignore a truth than to throw out vast paradigms and start afresh. If an individual sees only the biological birth resulting from sexual intercourse and the processes of biological life, he is sometimes content to look no further for the source of life. And if he does look further, he is easily blocked. His parameters for discovery are too

The Creator

restricted.

Nor is the answer offered by traditional religions acceptable. To say God created life is not enough. We must know what this God is and how he does what he does. To say it is heresy to ask these questions is as nonsensical as to not look both ways before crossing a street. Such a narrow focus on life will lead to little understanding and a lot of dangerous misinterpretation of very real facets of our environment. Until some resolution is made between the truths offered in religious texts and those known to science, there can be little progress in the quest for man's origins. For the scientist to say according to the Big Bang theory that the universe is only 15 billion years old is just a shade more productive than the Creationist who says it is only some 6000 years old. The scientist in this instance is just some 15 billion years closer to the truth and is offering a greater description of the Big Bang than the author of Genesis. The scientist's environmental assessment is more thorough and is based on greater knowledge. Yet it remains incomplete and is not yet definitive. There is more time in the past than a mere 15 billion years. That 15 billion years may well only be the first of many more billion years this present universal incarnation has already experienced.

These concepts may be more difficult to accept than they are to grasp, yet they are true. Man, as we know him, is a very recent creation. His history is a brief instant in the face of this universal incarnation, which itself is but an instant to the forces of time. The results of corporeal evolution are quite easily traced in our plane for there is a fossil record which provides indisputable evidence. Not so easy to trace in an empirical sense is the soul's evolution. It exists only in the memory of the soul and the only tool we have to trace it at this point is the human consciousness itself. Thus, we must invoke our old technique, the analysis of consistency, and explore as many soul histories as we can

Man's Unending Quest

to support the truths that are already obvious to those very souls. Though human beings are currently guided by a consistent type of soul, these souls are not exactly the same: their environmental influences have varied and so have their experiences. Yet there are many commonalities which will eventually spell themselves out to the collective human mind. When that happens, a paradigm of the human soul will emerge and will point us to the resolutions we seek for many of the spiritual truths we have so long promoted but have understood so little.

As humans, we stand at a crossroads in our history. We have achieved a level of understanding and knowledge that is unsurpassed by any prior generation. Still, we cling to old theories and ideas that are an extreme hindrance. We need only consider the revival of evangelical preaching to see how much humans still need to believe in a deity. Naturally, there are always those who are willing to dictate to them how they are to believe and how much they should pay for that belief. But the real purpose of religion is to provide a bridge between the fearful human mind and the entities who seek to guide mankind both for their own devices and for the good of our species. What happens on this plane is of importance primarily to this plane but the Karmic reality dictates that some of our actions influence other planes. Our souls will eventually join some of these higher worlds and obviously the residents therein will want compatible souls to join them. That means teaching us many of their ideals and preparing us for their Karmic existence. These guides are responsible for some of our less explicable or rational religious laws. When relating the laws to our world, we cannot necessarily see their value but they may have great value to us as a training procedure prior to joining a higher world. Yet at the same time, many of our seemingly senseless ideas are indeed senseless, the contructions of active human imaginations. Our task as an intelligent species,

The Creator

therefore, is to discover which is which.

If we reach back in time, we will see how easily and how thoroughly man distorts the truths he considers sacred. From the inception of Christianity, for instance, the religion as a whole has changed enormously. In the past two millenia, a great deal has been added to the Christian experience that does not directly relate to original teachings. Mostly, these additions are the results of the integration of Christianity into many other cultures. The other cultures add to the Christian teachings their own histories and cultural habits; the mainstream teachings also change over time according to interpretations of place and time. Thus, when we talk and teach of the absolute nature of our beliefs, we forget that our beliefs are not and never have been absolute. We embellish our religions, add to them ceremonies borrowed from other cultures and create doctrines designed more to serve human ends than to proclaim the will of higher entities. We above all seek to serve ourselves, not any god, and we should remember that. We are weak, bitter and emotional creatures who destroy readily for a cause. Too often, the cause we destroy for is the ultimate principle of love and brotherhood as represented in a religion.* Those destructions aren't the teachings of any deity or higher guide, but the outgrowth of a human animal possessed with intelligence he can scarcely control. We have had our truth suppressed in the name of truth and have learned to hate in the name of love. Such is not the work of the Creator; such is doubtfully even the work of man's creators. Such is only the work of man.

Of course, many adherents to the world's religions take

---

*At this writing, Islam, Judaism and Christianity are in particularly violent confrontation in Lebanon. The fight is not a religious one, but political. However, the battle lines are drawn on the basis of religious allegiances. Three traditions, therefore, that teach love and brotherhood confront each other in hate and bloodshed.

great umbrage when told their perceptions of truth are not absolute. The very nature of such doctrine is that it must be accepted without question. That is the heart of the destructive power in religious expansionism: fanatics believe it is better to destroy someone than to allow him his own choice of beliefs. They believe too strongly in the infallibility of their doctrine and, like the American bombings of Vietnamese villages which were intended to "save them from Communism", the efforts to save are often tragically and shamefully destructive. Yet despite the natural fanaticism of much of the human race, humanity has developed some great truths. Many of these truths have come from the technological advancements made by modern societies which are forcing the religions of the world to fall back and regroup. Many of the world's favorite doctrines have been torn asunder when scientific evidence forces people to acknowledge that some cherished tradition is only a less-than-true myth. Laws set down by religious orders in earlier times were made with no inclination of modern technology or the crowded conditions of this world. Thus, Catholicism still frowns on birth control, when the techniques of controlled population growth are necessary for the survival of the species. To assume that laws made in earlier days are absolute is to assume that those who made the laws were infallible. If they were infallible, they would have taken into account the realities of the future. Since the future still throws new situations at us, all of our truths and laws will have to evolve to account for the changing times. At no point in the past did the evolution of laws ever stop, the Bible itself being the best example of the evolution of law. Why, therefore, would any social group try to stop evolution now? For the most part, the religious societies of the world are left holding the tattered remnants of truths torn by time. Humanity has outgrown most of its religions. It must now forge new philosophies of life, a new harmonious Way.

The Creator

Our revitalized search for truth will lead us to less imperfect answers than before but still not perfect answers. We will still ask "Is there a God?" and will still be unable to answer ourselves satisfactorily. How can we answer ourselves, other than in our own individual terms? If there is a God, did he create man? And if he created man, why did he do so? He must have had a purpose. If that purpose, as Christianity and other religions suggest, is to serve God, hadn't we better learn exactly what is expected of us? And if this God is perfect, as Christianity suggests, why would perfection create imperfect humans to serve it? Wouldn't perfection be better served by perfect beings? Man's best proof that he was never perfect is that he is not perfect now: if ever perfect, how or why would he allow himself to become imperfect? Such a mistake would be impossible. Thus, the evolution of man is a theory that describes the process of how man has slowly emerged from his history to become as he is now. The contrary theories of primitive peoples are shadowed by lack of knowledge and environmental analysis. Their failing to arrive at perfect conclusions stems from their imperfect knowledge. They are, after all, only human.

Yet there are gods and divinities which, although not perfect, do have a great influence on human evolution. These entities have been present in our mythologies and religions for eons and will continue to manifest themselves. Although never perfect, they are perhaps closer to many ideals than humans are and they may indeed help us. The guides who have contacted me are perhaps little different than some of those who contacted the famous prophets of history: many people are contacted and never achieve any great reknown. The truths taught are never going to be absolutely the same, for the guides themselves differ in their experience. Far from there being a universal god guiding mankind, there are many specific entities who, though not omniscient, do know more about the universe than we do. As we come to understand more of the self and its relationship to environment, the forces governing the spiritual communications of humanity may be better understood. If we evolve far enough in our knowledge and wisdom, we may even fulfill the ancient teachings of our religions and join a higher world where our mentors and guides dwell. Although we may not know when this will happen, we can rest assured that the human species will not exist forever. In some number of years, perhaps hundreds or thousands, the race of souls using this form will move on to a higher experience, leaving the form to an encroaching race. At that point, the human biological species will take an exceptional turn in its evolution as the new race of souls establishes itself. We may never be able to precisely predict what those changes will be like but we can be certain that Humanity will not live on this earth until the close of time. Evolution won't permit it.

6

THE CROSSROADS OF MAN

Man has achieved a crossroads in his history. In this crossroads, he is prepared to marry the principles of his defined sciences with his less defined philosophies of existence. Essentially, the scientific and the philosophical represent the two arms of human knowledge, the two paths to understanding the human realm. Though related, the paths are distinct, for one strives to present truth through holistic theories picturing all of human reality and the other seeks to sequentially analyze that reality in painstaking depth, detail by detail, and thereby construct some overall view. To date, neither the holistic interpretations of truth offered by philosophers nor the carefully constructed paradigms of science have brought any full understanding of the human condition. Neither have fully defined the human being, let alone the environment which shapes him. The soul remains undiscovered.

The efforts of philosophers, both secular and religious, have long been oriented to defining the nature of human life in specific terms of the soul. Humanity's greatest philosophers have struggled with the questions of what drives the human flesh and have found no single persuasive answer other than to assume the existence of the soul. At best, this view, like any offered by the philosopher, is based on logical analyses of known and surmised truths which appear in some ways consistent and, to some at least, convincing. Yet ultimately, some faith is required before any philosophical truth may be accepted as fact because the benefit of proof remains at bay. On the other hand, science has also failed to present a persuasive explanation of these same forces. Though reaching far into the heart of material reality, science has not yet reached far enough to create a realistic theory as to what constitutes human life and intelligence. No science has reached far enough into the flesh to discover the soul or to even discover the fundamental principles of energy renewal responsible for the survival of life in temporal human flesh. Consequently, there are many humans who refuse to believe they each possess a soul, an energy-based consciousness which drives their existence. Unable to discover a material basis for the philosophical teaching that there is a soul, they reject the possibility that the material basis may still be there. They fail to consider that they may only be searching in the wrong place or using the wrong tools.

Science and philosophy, though often complementing each other, are also often opposed to each other in the restrictive practices of the various "schools of thought" which govern either at any given time or place. In some ways, the two are inseparable, for no scientific paradigm could be created without the imaginative context of philosophical endeavor; no philosophy could claim to be fact without scientific verification. Also, the religious-like fervor with which many scientists pursue a given theory can only be described as messianic, replacing the words "doctrine" and "dogma" with those considered more "objective". Yet few humans truly ascribe to objectivity, their interests and biases all showing in their work. As younger scientists reach into the future, the older order clings to the theories of an earlier day. Any new theory, like any new religion or philosophy, must fight its way into acceptance by capturing the will of

The Crossroads of Man

those who hold power. And those who hold power are seldom openly receptive to change. The physiological psychologist today is no more willing to accept that the soul could be rooted in something other than electro-chemical impulses than many earlier scientists believed heavier-than-air machines could fly. Though humanity looks for truth unceasingly, individual humans are all too often content to halt their quest when they become comfortable with a theory. If someone proves that theory wrong, many of us are too quick to persecute that individual for helping us learn: it is easier, perhaps, to spurn greater truths than to let them force lesser truths to fade into history.

When we finally allow new truths to emerge, we find we must reorganize much of what we think we know. New knowledge inevitably casts some of our present belief into disarray. Although some truths force their way into acceptance, others can be subverted indefinitely. To hold a belief, whether scientific or philosophical, is not to know an absolute truth, no matter how plausible that belief may appear. The belief only means that something has been assimilated and, for the moment, seems sound. At any point, new knowledge may prove this belief false, though the believer may strive desperately to hide from the knowledge in favor of his belief. Knowledge is acquired through perception and evaluation, not belief. It is something that is assimilated on the basis of observation and testing, a holistic assimilation of facts and theory which forces a certain level of acceptance. Though we may believe things that are not really true, belief relates only to a willingness to accept something as truth, having very little to do with facts.

Facts are the only true delineators of proved knowledge. Knowledge itself is very difficult to define though it is certain that something related to mathematical equation and thereby proved can truly be said to be known. There are other things that can be described as knowledge on the basis of such obvious truth that they cannot be denied. One such fact is our own existence. We know we exist because we do exist and, though fuel for much hypothetical debate, that statement cannot be justifiably disallowed. On that basis, therefore, we must accept that there is truth and definable fact somewhere that is responsible for everything else we perceive. On that basic premise, we build our entire perception of our known universe. Though our perceptions and our judgements are often faulty, we also know that the tests of time and consistency will allow us to cast off some of our less than true beliefs. If we seek to understand our universe, to *know* its facts and actual behavior, then we must be prepared to cast off many of our cherished falsehoods. If we persistently perceive a set of data, then we must ruthlessly test it. It is not enough merely to allow the most visible forces to rule as if they were facts. For example, our forefathers consistently perceived the sun and so do we. Our interpretation of the sun is vastly more sophisticated and factual than theirs in spite of our not being able to perceive any more of the sun with unassisted vision than they could. Our forefathers believed that the sun travelled across the sky over a stationary earth, for that is what the most obvious elements of perception told them. Then certain individuals took note of some anomalies which dispute that theory. It was not easy for them to change the perceptions of the majority, for the majority's perceptions were firmly fixed on the obvious. Yet the facts did not bear out the belief. Now we *know* the truth of the earth and the sun's movements, though there are undoubtedly facets of these movements we have to explore further. Although we are no more confident in our belief than our forefathers were in theirs, we are more confident in our facts: mathematical laws agree with the evidential material we have so far discovered.

The state of modern belief concerning the soul is no

The Crossroads of Man

more factual than that of our forefathers' belief in the movement of the sun. The majority of people believe in the soul only as told to believe in it by religion, a less than tangible experience. Because the soul is not obviously tangible to the human senses, there is no firm belief in what the soul is, only that it does indeed exist. And now that society moves away from many religious tenets that seem insubstantiable, belief in the soul wans. Scientists, no more able to perceive a soul than anyone else, seek proof in their accustomed manner, but have so far found nothing. For the most part, they are too wrapped up in the specifics of their chosen disciplines, none of which have any insight into the true nature of the soul. Consequently, the soul remains for the moment beyond discovery by scientific means. Rather than expand science to include this quest, as would be indicated by the current level of interest in human life, scientists choose instead to publicly ridicule any theory of the soul, despite their private religious or philosophical beliefs. They, in effect, practice two standards: a standard of belief for philosophical truth, which may include a religious-like interpretation of soul, and scientific truth, which will have no part of it. Rather than admit their own religious leanings (though not all scientists are religious), they reject the experiential evidence of millions of people who have encountered phenomena that go unexplained by science. Yet these people do not try to subvert or compromise the scientific community, as many scientists blatantly assert; they merely wish to understand the things that have undeniably happened to them. The few selected disciplines of accepted science having failed them, some individuals always prove determined and tenacious enough to create a new discipline and earn acceptance.

As much as the quest for soul, humans need a quest for god. Every identifiable human society which has left a record of a philosophy of existence has maintained some form of belief in a god or gods. Though god is not a proved fact, the idea retains a powerful base of belief. Such belief should not remain unchallenged by those who purportedly seek to define human existence or the universe. To maintain such a powerful belief, a set of facts must exist to support it. Even though the interpretation may not be correct as humans have currently defined their gods, further analysis may point to definible facts. Just as the sun was a perceived reality that required more sophisticated approaches to ferret out its truth, so is the notion of god. To some, the physical search of the cosmos has answered their quest; seeing nothing, sensing nothing, the quest is complete. Yet for the majority of humans, the quest is not complete. The lack of evidence for a god does not prove an absense of god, merely an absense of evidence. If the search into the heart of the atom or the flinging of sensitive equipment into the cosmos does not resolve the question, the search need only be extended to new areas. Somewhere, there exists an answer and no answer concerning the infinite nature of the universe can be defined using paradigms restricted to finite disciplines. If no evidence is found to prove a theory and none is found to disprove it, the quest should not be abandoned. To do so is the equivalent of Columbus sailing to America in quest of India and stopping there, saying nothing lies beyond. The quest is merely incomplete.

As our religions and philosophies have long encouraged us to do, we should extend our quest for life to the world of the mystic. Once we come to understand the forces that drive our consciousness, we will have opened the door to the worlds of the mystical — and our hidden gods. We have little understanding of these other worlds, save for the wisdom passed down through the ages which in many instances is little more accurate than the early perceptions of the movements of the sun. Most of us, because of the superstitious teachings of our forefathers, have a great fear

The Crossroads of Man

of what we may find there: we fear the wrath of gods, the scourge of demons and the torment of gnomes, goblins and malevolent spirits. Childish fears, perhaps, but fears nonetheless. The world of the occult has been portrayed as a fearsome thing, its painted rituals coloring our imaginations with a fury we pass on through witchdoctors, sorcerers and magicians. When our known sciences fail us, we always reach to the vast realms of the unknown, the occult, for succor. Though many of our scientists still sneer at the word occult, many occult forces have become recognized facts. Faith healing, for one, is gaining ground in the medical world as medical doctors finally begin to understand the abilities of the human body to heal itself.

We don't understand the forces of spiritualism. We have religions that seek to explain these forces as the whims and fancies of gods; we have satanists and sorcerers who use cloudy rituals to fog our minds. Yet it is the fear inspired by the ritual that often holds the power in religion or sorcery; ritual affects the perceptions and perceptions stimulate the reorganization of conscious energies. Though it is possible to tap weird forces, few sorcerers or religious mystics have any real understanding of their art. They merely act in age-old (or recently imagined) rituals that supposedly hold power. The suggestive power of ritual is its only strength, having a base in common experience which allows individuals to convince themselves that the ritual is strong. Otherwise all power comes from the consciousnesses of any living entities which may be participating in the rituals. The power of suggestion is often quite mighty when the energy of the mind fuses itself with some of the energies of the soul. The results can sometimes seem magical or miraculous, propelling mystic or religious belief. The soul, breaking through to the mind more purely than it ever has before, is suddenly able to organize a vast effect on the organism it has never had before. Other souls, from the human

Man's Unending Quest

Afterlife or elsewhere, may join in the effect breached by a single soul to help heal a body or to effect some conscious realization. The forces of combined will are the same as the will of one entity but sometimes stronger. To modern man, these words may seem strangely similar to those offered by the sorcerer, not convincing at all to the scientist. Yet if we analyzed the soul as we do the atom and then constructed school curricula based on what we learned as we do for chemistry and mathematics, then the soul would not seem mystical at all. For us, the mystical nature arises from its unknown and unfamiliar aspects. Since we cannot understand the material forces which are at work, we call them "spiritual", "supernatural" or "magic". We translate something real into something that can only be dealt with through our superstitious natures.

Our failing to allow our perception of the unknown to transcend silly notions of "supernatural" is the result of our unwillingness to admit to ourselves that there are vast ranges of material existence about which we know little or nothing, save what our myths and fairytales tell us. We interpret material reality as the material reality we have so far defined in mathematical or atomical terms. Once atomical theory is excluded from human knowledge on earth, there is very little else that can be forged into a cohesive theory. In short, when it comes to anything besides the nature of atomical particles and their effects, both macroscopically and microscopically, we are hopelessly ignorant. Outside of atomical theory, all we have to regard as human knowledge are vague notions of life-after-death and of gods, angels and other semi-realized entities. When we can't define these other elements of material reality in terms of atomical theory, we label them "superstition" and either nonsense or nondefinable. We cease our quest, Columbus beached on the shores of Europe before leaving the quay. Granted, the atom and all its forms may be the

The Crossroads of Man

single greatest force in our in-flesh lives, but is it the only force? What of all the other vast reaches of the universe? Don't we even care enough to open our minds to them? Everything in the universe that we choose to define as real is a part of the material universe, even gods and angels. If that is what we choose to call something that is real, we can't just pretend that it is not definible or the result of superstition: if the beliefs came to be as pervasive as they are in human society, something other than mere random chance put them there. An analysis of existing documentation concerning non-atomical reality presents many consistencies which could lead us to defining genuine laws. Since many writers before me (Alan Watts and Carl Jung are two) have already spelled out some of these consistencies, I present here a working paradigm which can be methodically tested. In essence, there is little in this book that hasn't been presented to man many times before in religious and mystical teaching and a good deal of it has been experienced by many humans. This paradigm is merely a consolidation of much that is already known and is presented without a lot of religious or mystical jargon that many people find distasteful.

Despite the jargon of many other documents and although much of the belief of the religions and mystical orders of the world will be proved false, there is no reason not to treat each of these beliefs as something that offers some insight to truth. Whatever defined truth can be found in any belief system can be used as a springboard to higher learning. If a belief cannot be assimilated into current knowledge, perhaps only further information is required to make an isolated fact seem less contradictory to knowledge. There is much that we could learn merely by plumbing the depths of human consciousness as many mystics try to do. That we seldom take advantage of the teachings of mystics is perhaps best related to the flurry of interest caused by a visit to town by a showman hypnotist. As the showman performs wonderful feats of memory and hypnosis, people are invariably impressed and wish to follow his example. However, without training and discipline of the exact nature necessary to be successful, few pursue their new interest. Of all the people in the audience, perhaps one or two or three may ever learn much of the showman's skills, if any. Yet if people were dedicated and were widely taught the techniques, human memory skills and powers of consciousness could be vastly improved. The three main forces that stop us are doubt, laziness and lack of organized direction.

In a further pursuit of knowledge, we must lose our fear of knowledge. Much of our societal training has forced us to fear the truths we would like to understand better. We are told to accept them unquestioningly, to not doubt their greater wisdom. Yet we are not told *why* we should not question the truths we are presented in religion when so many of them are self-contradictory. We find ourselves rejecting whole facets of our experience because we cannot agree with the symptoms of that experience: we throw the baby out with the bathwater. On the other hand, progressive elements within religion allow truths to be questioned and invariably the traditional interpretations and belief structures erode as logic and modern knowledge tear away at the beliefs of earlier times. And something whole remains that is very valuable indeed: the core of the belief system. In any religion, the core beliefs are those that are common to all mankind, though specific elements of doctrine may disagree. The brotherhood of mankind is a concept that is a core belief in Christianity and one that is universal to human-kind. None of the atrocities committed by man against himself should deter any of us from believing in the justness of that concept. As a philosophy of human life, it steers us straight down the path to all the higher glories promised by religions but which they communicate ineffectively and confusedly.

The Crossroads of Man

We confuse notions of the brotherhood of man with the brotherhood of Christians or Catholics or Baptists. Yet because we sometimes fail to act in the manner taught us by a great ideal, need we strive any less for that ideal? While mankind squabbles over *how* to believe in universal brotherhood, the ideal is hidden.

It is ignorance which forces humans to kneel to the mercy of warlords and priests. Traditionally, the efforts of the world's power structures have been to keep the masses ignorant, to not allow them to understand the forces which govern them. It was only a century ago that a few industrialized countries grudgingly granted the masses universal education. Even at that, the ruling hegemonies were sorely appalled and fought viciously against the liberalization. Liberalism has always been a pressing force of human evolution (the Laws of Moses were more liberal than those that went before; the guidelines of Christ more liberal still), yet standing orders have also always tried to inhibit the force. The techniques used to subdue a people struggling to be freer have always been fear and indoctrination. People who fear for their safety are inhibited from tackling the power structure and those who can be taught to support the power structure are less trouble still.

The governmental forces of man have instilled a very deep fear (sometimes a great resentment) of authority. The Christian is taught to fear his omnipotent god; the communist peasant taught to fear the absolute power of his regime; the occultist teaches the initiate to fear the powers he seeks to control. In such cases, the individual is encouraged on pain of great punishment to fear the power structure so that he will not challenge it. He is taught of the all-knowing power that can crush him at any time, during life or after, so he must beware. If taught thoroughly enough, the fear is so pervasive that rebellion is nipped in the bud. Yet if allowed to understand the forces that govern him, he learns that there are weaknesses in the governing power structures and their ideas; thus the determined and courageous rebel can effect changes if mass support can be gained. But too often mass support leads only to another hegemony which plays about with a slightly different set of ideas that are supposed to be equally perfect as those they displaced. Sometimes, however, there is a true liberalizing of the society and though perfection will never emerge from any such change, vast improvements in the conditions of the masses may indeed be achieved. And that is often worth the risk of rebellion.

Too much of our human intellectual history has been wasted in fear. We have sullied and blockaded too much of our minds with useless fears that human governments, both secular and religious, have learned to instill to gain control. Fear, however, is an element of the primal human being and is a weapon for survival. Our fears began when we were the very crude and timid creatures of the forests and plains who failed to understand the forces that drove the world. We feared thunderstorms because they were noisy and unpleasant and sometimes deadly. We feared the droughts that destroyed our basis of livelihood. We feared all the natural forces of disease, starvation and predators that could strike us down with little warning. We learned to fear the night itself, to fear its darkness as something that held terrors for us we couldn't imagine. Then we began to imagine these terrors: though we perhaps drew on the innate knowledge of the soul for the substance of these fears, fear itself was the motivation. Darkness became the symbol of fear, and because we hate to be afraid, we made it the symbol of evil as well. Even today, knowing full well that there is nothing in the dark that isn't there in the light, many humans fear the dark. It does no good for someone who is not afraid of the dark and comes to no harm from that lack of fear to reassure the one who fears: the fear itself is the controlling

The Crossroads of Man

power. Rationality does not always reign.

Fears taught by religious or other philosophy are no more rational. It doesn't matter to the Christian that a Buddhist holds little fear of death because Buddhism teaches that death is a positive element in the renewal of life. The Buddhist would likely scoff at the idea of Hell. Yet the Christian who is morbidly afraid of death because he was threatened as a child with eternal damnation because he uttered the blasphemies his parents taught him will not be solaced. The fear need not be reasoned, it need not be based on a reality; it only needs to exist. We have found no Hell with our mineshafts and drill bits and to the logically minded, that offers some reassurance without ending all fear. There is still the possibility to the fearful mind that Hell is only hidden in some other way, waiting for them. The fear runs before logic, creating its own justification. Only the ultimate knowledge of what happens to souls after the death of the flesh will ever reassure that person and even then his fear will be a buffer against the truth.

To understand something does not necessarily remove all fear but it does help. In my personal experience, I have managed to purge myself of most of the irrelevant fears taught me by my relatively enlightened form of Christian upbringing. Even so, I still have traces of irrational fears which I know have little base in reality. Consequently, I sympathize greatly with those who are taught a less forgiving style of Christianity. There is a basis for the Christian belief in the torment of the soul but the religion has parodied it into a fearsome thing far worse than it is. The basis for the teaching is only that a soul can cause itself much anguish, most of it self-inflicted, when it has caused harm while in flesh. For some, the anguish may seem interminable but is definitely never eternal. However, in the graphic way these truths have been interpreted down through the past two millenia, a tradition of inflexibility has evolved which should not have been. Our attitudes, whether those of the supposedly unbiased scientist or the self-righteous fundamentalist, are forged by the ideas we have been trained to accept. In the Christian world, that means we fail to see the flexible nature of evolving lifeforms and the ability of a soul to recover from its past wrongs.

Societal training is the greatest force in the mind's awareness. As well as the religious myths I was taught as a child, I learned of many equally fallacious notions which terrified me even more. Tales of vampires and the "undead" made me frightened of the dark. Even as an adult, reading Bram Stoker's *Dracula* evoked some fearsome nightmares. Human society is so steeped in such superstition that it is nearly impossible for a young child in the Western world to grow up and not "know" that a silver bullet kills a werewolf or a wooden stake driven through the heart kills a vampire. Though we can be certain that werewolves and vampires are not real phenomena on this plane, do we have any equal certainty that our penchant for such tales is not based on some innate awareness that doesn't stem from this world? Though the tiny vampire bats of South America may well provide fuel for the imaginative creation of a story such as Bram Stoker's, how can we assess the powerful emotions and gut reactions it evokes? People create imaginative stories all the time but only certain ones seem to grasp a broad acceptance, as if many of us are compelled to accept them. Writers often speak of this responsive chord and long to touch it. Some do but most don't. Those who do provide other writers such as Alan Watts and Carl Jung with more subject matter to analyze.

We must understand that though there are very real limits to this world, many other worlds have different limitations. We cannot be harmed in this life by "ghosts" (really only certain discarnate souls who touch this plane for reasons of their own) but we can be driven in paroxyms

The Crossroads of Man

of fear to do ourselves much harm. Most often, the tales of ghosts are only the imaginings of a frightened person in an empty house but sometimes that person does encounter a soul who wishes to communicate. Very seldom is that communication a visual one, though some in-flesh humans do have the ability to see many forms of apparitions. Likewise, some discarnate souls have the ability to project themselves in a manner visible to in-flesh humans of ordinary visual talents. When such a thing happens, the in-flesh human is usually too scared (or dumbfounded) to make any sense out of it or to effect any useful communication. The incident then becomes another campfire tale and adds to the base of experience which ensures that belief in other worlds never ceases. Yet that belief also remains a very hypothetical one to those who don't directly experience something from another world and is of very little use to all concerned.

As long as we fear the souls of our departed friends (does a character named Scrooge come to mind?), how can they approach us in friendly communication? Those who are inclined to believe in fairytales are often inclined to accept the junk that goes along with them, including irrational fears. Our very fears lead us into stupid actions sparked by superstitious imaginings twisted by the tall tales of childhood. We fear demons from the other side and therefore some souls are tempted to play nasty tricks. We fear our gods and therefore imagine them to lay down all sorts of fearsome laws, then imagine more fearsome punishments for those who break the imagined laws. When all is said and done, we have never in thousands of years of intellectual guidance by higher entities learned to control our interactions with lifeforms from other planes of existence. Instead, superstition guides our actions. Because we possess souls, our minds are never quite allowed to forget that the soul exists. It is the relationship between mind and base soul which prompts the evocative reactions to certain stimuli: just like we all have our personal interests which are based in the soul, we all have common interests. The soul tries in many ways through the course of the incarnation to control the mind but does not often have great enough power. The mind does have a certain autonomy though it is far from independent. Like a sovereign nation which interacts with its neighbors, the mind must draw from the soul some influences to survive. Too much influence, however, and the mind is also in danger. Thus, the ebb and flow of human awareness strive to strike a balance, a natural harmony that will allow both the mind and the soul to function in reasonably efficient ways.

The training of the mind, based as it is on the sometimes foolish interpretations of truth forged by a society of minds (that is, in-flesh human society), often conflicts with the truth of the soul. Though the soul does strive to right these wrongs, the soul cannot teach the mind directly except through memory and experience. The limiting factor in this case is the ability of the mind to assimilate truth. If the soul could open the gates of the middle conscious and force all its knowledge through, the mind would capsize. The mind just could not handle the sudden influx of truth; it must be built, like all things worth building, slowly and carefully. Thus, it is the task of the mind to learn. Just as one soul can teach another soul or one mind can teach another mind (the basic learning processes of, respectively, the soul-world and the in-flesh world), a soul can teach a mind. The technique involved is very similar but does require an essential cooperation between the soul of one entity and the mind of the other. Most souls have the patience and knowledge to indulge in such teaching processes but as we have found in our world, many minds are not willing to learn. Or at least, most minds learn very selectively. Thus, the misconceptions of society get carried from one gener-

The Crossroads of Man

ation of minds to another, with the combined efforts of all souls only marginally guiding the species to higher understandings of basic truths. If one human being puts aside his acceptance of superstition, he may teach his children the same way. All too often, the superstitions of one generation are passed down to the next.

Any belief should be well tested before it is passed on to children. We should test our religions and political beliefs as thoroughly as we have tested certain fairytales. If we find a belief that has an immediate foundation in fact, then we should cherish that belief. If, however, we find one that has no apparent basis, we should reserve judgement on it and carry it with us only as a possibility of truth. We should not reject something that is neither provable nor unprovable but merely hold it carefully as something to be studied further. Many of our beliefs have been carried forward as the banners of ultimate truth. Countless people have died over the supposedly infallible nature of the Pope or Marx, yet both have proved to be very fallible. The belief that "Thou shalt not kill" has been sullied for thousands of years even though its worth and value is as obvious as good health and happiness. And humans still cling to less worthy beliefs to the exclusion of good health and happiness. Why? Most humans who hold fanatic beliefs don't even understand why. They merely hold the beliefs and find their justification wherever they can. The need to press the beliefs upon others is often seen as a justification and cause in itself. If others come to the cause, willingly or not, then the cause seems even more just. Consider the opposing strategies of the Soviet Union and the United States. Their strategies are opposing but not opposite. Both practice the same self-righteous domination of their client states and use the same tactics of subversion, force, indoctrination and bribery. None of these methods is founded in justice or decency but the propaganda of both sides stresses very clearly the intention of the dominating powers to uphold justice and decency. The fact that both gather the support of their populations is testimony only to the further use of subversion, force, indoctrination and bribery. Even in the U.S., where citizens have somewhat more freedom than Soviet citizens, the price of this freedom is the willingness to turn a nearly blind eye to such travesties as the U.S. involvement in Central America. Though voices in the U.S. are raised in protest, very few people are willing to take an active risk in opposing the government. If they did, another Kent State University tragedy would probably occur, the indoctrinated National Guard doing its duty without question of moral purpose.

Our highest ideals are thoroughly colored with blood. Every emancipation of man has been the result of some long and often vicious struggle. Power structures do not like to change the ideals by which they govern; to do so is to admit their earlier imperfections. To admit imperfection is to admit weakness and that leads many to question why they follow such an imperfect government. And too often the emancipation is bought with blood, the bitter fruit of impatience. As a power base begins to erode, the power structure begins its struggle to regain its strength. Heavier oppression leads to more discontent and eventually a critical point is reached: emancipation is bought at any price. Such emancipation carries a greater price than that of winning: it, too, must maintain power and if it bought power with blood, it will keep power with blood. The doctrine of emancipation becomes a new doctrine of oppression.

The teachings of our gentlest prophets aid us little when we decide to establish power centers. The prophetic teachings are often used as devices of destruction much more effectively than guns or bombs. Propaganda is a far more effective recruitment tool than impressment gangs; a willing fanatic will fight much harder than an unwilling conscript.

The Crossroads of Man

If we judge our highest truths by what man has done with them, they will not seem so high at all. But if we manage to look beyond the failings of man, we can see these truths as they are: guides to a better way of life. Though the lure of war drums is more thrilling than the quietude of peace, the conflict gains little but great sadness for those harmed in it. More, peace is the reconstructive force which renews a society ravaged by war. The war itself builds nothing; it only tears down. Though the destruction may clear the way for more construction, peacefully planned reconstruction is a far more productive means of allowing the future to find its place in the present. There is no need in any society for the mindless destruction of a war, yet many powerful humans are unwilling to step aside to allow more just ways of life to come into existence.

Violent rebellion often seems necessary to spark real progress. When such violence erupts, the guides of various humans will undoubtedly help humans on both sides: the aid of higher entities is bought through personal favor, not necessarily a cause. No society or army is completely just in its cause. Only propaganda convinces anyone that such is the case. Thus, it is arguable that in war there is no "right" side, just sides that are less wrong.

If our guides, those entities we have always chosen to call gods, have persistently taught us the ways of peace, why is war such an omnipresent force? Could it be that they are just as powerless as we are to stop war? There is much speculation possible as to the motives of these higher entities in guiding us but we know (if we accept the consistent documentation of their efforts as evidence for those efforts) that higher entities have interfered with human wars. In religious books such as the Bhagavad Gita and the Bible, wars spurred on and even fought and won by gods are sickening in their bloodiness. The Bible even goes to the extent of counting the dead. Supposedly millions of people who stood in the way of a migrating tribe were killed. In many of our mythologies, gods fight among themselves: consider those of Christianity (Lucifer cast from heaven), ancient Greece (the rivalries of Mount Olympus) and North America (the powerful Thunderbird overcoming lesser gods). While leading a single warrior or an army or a nation to war, why would these same gods often teach the moral virtues of brotherhood, peace and good fellowship? The Christian god is said to have sent his son to teach humanity brotherhood; the gods and spirits of North American native mythology teach the moral virtues of loving all that exists, an act of love for an animal often leading the warrior to a guardian spirit represented by that animal. These guardian gods and spirits invariably work through a single human in these legends, with that human providing leadership to his fellows. Why does a god teaching love and brotherhood join in any crusade or cause on behalf of the chosen human or his people?

The answer is that even though these higher guides may know more of the ideals they teach than we do, they too have yet to achieve perfection. They may, for all we know, be carrying their own wars to our world and setting various tribes or nations of humans at each other's throats. Or, they may merely wish to help an individual and his people overcome some oppressive force and choose the expedient method of violent overthrow: peaceful evolution is very slow. We can speculate endlessly as to the motives of any foreign entity for becoming involved in our affairs but at this point we have very little information on which to build; as our myths and religions indicate, these higher entities are very close-lipped and jealous about their own affairs. Whatever their motives, we can be certain that the only way we can learn about them is to study them, as no doubt they have been studying us. Our task, therefore, must lead us to ask questions of the entities that have long posed as our gods. Since we perceive weaknesses in what we know of them, how can we be certain, as some of our religions try to convince us, that any god can be infallible? At best, they can only be less fallible than us and the documentation we have compiled about our gods testifies to that: no perfect god created imperfect men; even the protected Achilles had his vulnerable heel.

If we seek to study truth or human nature, then we must question all aspects of it. If there are aspects of it that are unpleasant or threatening or even of doubtful validity, we must still effect honest study. If we test the truth of religions and fear the vengeance of a powerful god, perhaps we should ask why any god that represents justice would be vengeful. Do we want to follow vengeful gods? Yet if some other entity wishes to teach us a better way, what harm is there in considering it? If we wish to adopt it, we may do so. No punishment awaits our souls if we don't. We needn't force ourselves and others to accept any idea at the pain of great war or mass death. There is little or no justice in such tragedy. It is far more defensible to put a good idea to the test of logical minds and if it seems sound to pursue it. No god will sit in judgement of those who try and those who don't.

The individual soul must guide itself in what it is prepared to accept. More, it should guide itself in how it interacts with its higher guides. There is no need to worship them, though every lifeform deserves respect. Our religions tell of the great power and vengeance exercised by many gods. For that reason, we often fear what lies beyond the death of the flesh. Yet that is a great sadness, for teaching should not be done on pain of punishment. Still, when unsophisticated minds are involved, such as children or primitive humans, the threat of pain is sometimes the only means of capturing attention. Some entities have undoubtedly used the technique to great effect and it has become the basis of much religious conformity. On the other hand, the tendency in recent years has been the emancipation of people and the loosening of doctrine. Despite throwbacks like the Ayotollahs of Iran, the world's religious philosophies are far more forgiving of individual thought than ever before. The emancipation of the mind is one of the greatest steps in the emancipation of man.

The emancipation of man is a gradual thing. We are being emancipated, slowly and surely, from our animal nature. While in this animal flesh and dependent on it for the evolution of our souls, we cannot transcend our animal nature entirely. Yet we can *nearly* transcend it and at that point, perhaps our higher guides will accept us (as souls) into their worlds. We will have then left behind our human flesh and the reincarnation cycle of this plane forever. Until then, we must work here at bettering ourselves and our collective societies. While we do that, we will be guided by higher entities in more ways than we know or imagine, and usually without ever realizing it. Or, we will continue to give thanks to anonymous gods, without even caring to delve into the nature of those gods and learn how closely they are related to us as souls. They are a part of the geometric progression of life within this planet, as we are, and they are a part of our experience. Because that is so, we are also a part of their experience. Our formative influence on each other, like the formative influences shared by a soul and corporeal body, are as infinite as the actions of man and god in an infinite environment. In such a relationship, we needn't worship our elevated relatives. We need only understand them as they must understand us.

Thus, we stand at a crossroads. We can learn more of these gods and the so-called mystical effects that they have on our lives or we can ignore them. We have achieved a point of evolution where either action is possible. No matter how many of us follow the road of ignorance, we can be certain

The Crossroads of Man

that it will eventually join the road of knowledge again. When it does, we will have learned a great deal and will have been taught by those who have sought to follow the road of knowledge every step of the way. When we meet at that next crossroads, it will be with a fuller understanding of the word god and with a greater appreciation for the myriad of entities that have touched our lives without our full realization. We will then have outgrown our need for "gods" and have grown into a new realm of friendship.

7

THE CULTIVATION OF MAN

Man is a cultivated species. Like many of the domesticated animals of the human world, man himself is the product of careful engineering on the part of higher entities. These entities have largely selfish aims: as the souls now using the human form will eventually emerge into their worlds, they have an interest in shaping their future neighbors. Their interest is not as callous as the term "engineering" may at first indicate, the contacts between man and higher guides often being very loving in the truest sense of the word. We have built this notion of love into our religious experiences and have seldom come to understand the word we parrot so faithfully. In fact, we confuse it with the personal sort of loves we share with our spouses, our children and other family. We do not comprehend what our guides mean by love any more than we understand the concept of God.

The cultivation results from man's likeness (in terms of his soul-nature) with certain higher orders of entity. These entities, like the gods described in human religions, often take a personal interest in an individual and that individual then extends the effect of such an influence to other humans. In that activity, the guides of these other humans may take a hand, using their subliminal abilities to guide their respective human contacts to perform cooperative (or obstructive or indifferent, for that matter) acts. The guidance of an individual human being is seldom fully consciously realized by the human mind but if it is, it is usually interpreted by that mind as a message or "sign" from a divinity or god, depending, of course, on the individual's religion. For those who follow no religion and profess to believe in no god, the reaction to an external influence may be interpreted as "chance", "coincidence" or "fate", several very carefully nonreligious terms. If the contact with a higher entity (or any inexplicable phenomenon) is too thoroughly obvious to be sloughed off casually, many individuals suddenly "see the light", are "born again" or otherwise conscript themselves to a religious faith. The presence of something entirely alien to their expected experience is too great to ignore and the result is a baffled mind that grabs at the closest available explanation: religion. Some people, too, merely carry the experience with them as an unexplained event that profoundly affects their interpretation of static reality. In all cases, the "god" that speaks on occasion to men is not a singular party that knows all and sees all but is merely one of many billions of higher-order souls who find their own fates somehow linked with those of individual human beings.

Human mystics often speak of unseen or other-worldly guides. These spiritual mentors, as we call them, find that their task in life involves in part the teaching of human beings. Some individual humans lend themselves more readily to spiritual instruction than others, the level of spiritual awakening any human acquires depending on his evolutionary status. Some humans prefer to learn more of material lessons than spiritual ones, finding their truth more comfortably spent in study of, say, animal nature than mystical knowledge. Such is fine, for there are many others who are more than willing to take up the task of furthering man's spiritual development. Any student of metaphysics

The Cultivation of Man

is familiar with the basic principles of mind over matter, mental enhancement and "consciousness raising". Although "consciousness raising" is not a technically precise term, it is graphically illustrative. For many of us, the presence of higher intelligences is something we acknowledge only in terms of religion or not at all: for the true metaphysician, the presence of higher guides is part of life's practical experience. For the metaphysician, establishing a contact with a higher world is a matter of course; for the bulk of humanity, the lessons of higher worlds are learned through others. The human mind, because it is a fragile and delicate thing, is not always allowed to be fully a part of the metaphysical spectrum. Unfortunately, that truth breeds many skeptics, those who never have blatant metaphysical experiences even when they put heartfelt effort into a spiritual quest. Too many other matters seem to press inwards on the person who only devotes a spotty effort in quest of metaphysical truth: the experiences thus gleaned are either unsatisfactory, temptingly incomplete or thoroughly inconclusive. Like any other reasonable discipline, the quest for metaphysical truth requires discipline, diligent study and a lot of mind-bending realizations. Too many quasi- or would-be metaphysicians find discouragement in their first efforts, after making little or no effort to prepare for the quest. No doctor sets up shop without adequate medical training and internship, nor does any true quest for truth bear honest fruit without proper training and learned skills.

Our minds are often the blocking factors in the quest for metaphysical experience. If a person is not willing to experience shocking and frightening truths, or worse yet, to discover his own imperfections (many of us really aren't), the quest for a metaphysical guide will likely fail, at least as far as the mind-conscious is concerned. The mind is only a part of the experience of the Soul, alive for a given incarnation then blended into the greater experience of many past incarnations. There is much activity in the world of the soul to which the human mind is oblivious. As we stand in front of a shop window, we do not often realize that our souls are in contact with many realms of consciousness. While we look longingly at a particularly appealing article of clothing, the soul may be actively organizing many facets of our experience for the years to come. The article of clothing may indeed figure prominently in a coming event but chances are its presence or absence would have no great effect on the course of a lifetime. If the article of clothing does figure prominently in a coming event, the soul most likely foresaw the purchase of that article years before, perhaps even before that incarnation. Usually, however, the soul does not concern itself much with the petty adornments of the body, for it is interested in a more holistic perspective of life. It chooses to guide the mind to the things that are important to a given incarnation; but the various hours of leisure time or amusements of the mind are left to the mind, though the mind's interests are very often integral to those of the soul. They are, after all, part of the same integrated consciousness.

The soul need not guide the mind continuously. It does have a conscious presence associated with the mind during the periods we call the "waking state" (the soul is actually far more "awake" than our minds can ever hope to be), but the presence is only marginal. The soul is, for the most part, aware of what the mind is thinking and preparing to make the body do and a cutover to instinctive reaction can occur in an instant. The soul largely guides the mind through instinctive or "gut" feelings which we often have trouble identifying or putting to words. While the soul is submerged beneath the mind's "waking state", it is usually in communication with other souls, setting up coming events and experiences. The soul must engineer most of these

The Cultivation of Man

experiences on an ongoing basis, though most, if not all, major experiences are carefully planned just prior to the incarnation. The soul is a remarkable device for holistic analysis: it can predict the future in a very precise pictogram, seeing all events that will happen in the near future. Yet it still must engineer the events by causing the necessary elements of that experience to come together. In short, no plan bears fruit if no one implements it.

Thus, since other souls guiding other people provide the basis for the developing experience, the soul must communicate with those about to join in the experience. The "scene", like a well-planned movie scene, is planned a few days, weeks or even months before it occurs. The people involved may back out or change but the essential experience remains the same. If the soul is especially skilled, it may be able to tell which individuals will not appear as expected and make alternate arrangements. As the old saying goes, "the best laid plans of mice and men often go awry". The same holds true for souls. Nonetheless, the plot for the lifetime rarely changes. If there are major failures, the soul has foreseen them but hopes to learn enough from them to succeed with a future effort. No incarnation is a total failure; all add something useful to a soul's experience. When a soul faces a particularly eventful or important life (relative to most human lives), there are many other souls who will join in the efforts of guiding the body and mind. Other souls have the same basic abilities to communicate with a human mind as the base soul beneath that mind; the mechanisms for communication are the same, but the communicants are different. The communicant need not be another human soul, though it often is. Often, it is a selected guide for that human, one that has a special skill or skills for aiding that human. Seldom do these guides present themselves clearly to the human mind: that would necessitate explaining far more than the mind could assimilate. Consider the evangelical Christian, for example. How many such fundamentalist Christians would be willing to consider that the "voice" speaking to their consciousness was other than the Christian god? Would the evangelist be willing to forego his evangelical style of preaching and adopt the Way of the higher worlds he often mistakenly calls Heaven? Our minds simply fail to understand the basic principles of the soul's relationship with its universe, always striving to interpret the soul's experience in terms of the mind's experience. The mind cannot help but do that, for that is how it functions. Yet as a mechanism for deriving absolute truth, it leaves far too much to be desired. Opinion and belief too often get in the way of objective understanding.

Our minds can recognize the basic elements of the soul, yet the intricacies are lost. Too much, especially, is lost when concepts from the soul are translated into human language. The soul does not think as the mind does. Instead, it assimilates a holistic impression of impulses that surround it, without straining to sort them out strand by strand as does the mind. Thus, while the mind struggles to put words to a description of the color yellow, the soul merely assimilates its meaning in much the way the mind perceives the color. Rather than a relatively meaningless vision of a color, the soul's translation of the color includes an immediate analysis of its surrounding influences. It can perceive the color, as does the mind, but at the same time identifies and assimilates how that color changes its surroundings, how its intensification would cause further alterations and how its absence would affect the immediate ecosystem. The human mind merely sees yellow.

Language further stilts the mind as human speech cannot possibly vocalize the vast complexities of the universe. At best, we can strive for common understanding by attaching words (symbols) to elements of common experience. Without common experience, no two individuals

The Cultivation of Man

could communicate through language in even the simplest terms. How could you describe the color yellow to someone who has never seen it? How do you describe mountains to plains-dwellers who have never seen more than the mildest hillock? The answer, of course, is that you use the hillock as a reference point and strive to describe through other symbolic means the differences between the hillock and the mountain. The understanding imparted through such a process will undoubtedly be vague and misinterpreted, but some of the general idea will get across. It is thus that humans have been learning from their higher guides. For centuries, man has learned higher ideals in terms he could understand as shepherds and warriors. Now, man is becoming far more sophisticated, able to understand far more complex ideas with the aid of mathematics than he could in less developed ages. Knowledge that could be transferred from a more developed intellect to the simple shepherds of Abraham's time had to be distilled to its most basic elements and given to a likely individual. Sometimes the message took root, sometimes it didn't. The truths we see in the Bible, for example, are those that have been given to simple people, passed on orally for generations and eventually transcribed and translated many times. Much has been lost, much more added. At this point, it is very difficult to say what parts of the Bible are the historical chronicles of man and which are the teachings of higher mentors. The best way we can tell is to analyze the common traits of the Bible with other religious texts and note the basic similarities. When we look at religious documents in that perspective, a pattern definitely emerges.

Communications from higher entities are not often well received. Usually they are exceptionally garbled by the time the human mind comes to have some understanding of them. The efforts of the soul to transmit them to the mind are often abject failures: the mind is a receiving device and it receives soul impulses poorly. It can achieve certain holistic impressions but is very weak in interpreting them, both because of the human requirements of linear analysis and the translation to language. If a message is to be transmitted from a soul to the mind, whether from that same human's soul or from another soul, the mind must be able to clear a path through the middle conscious so that it may be clearly received. The middle conscious, which exists as a physical barrier between the in-flesh mind and the base soul, protects the mind from unwanted soul impulses but at the same time garbles many valid messages. Like a faulty buffer in a computer, the middle conscious filters the messages from the soul's level of consciousness before they reach the mind. The middle conscious is the level in which superstition and other beliefs of the mind interfere with genuine knowledge of the soul. Though the soul knows the human interpretation of Hell is vastly misapplied, it can often do little to get past the mind's fears of such an awful punishment. The myth breeds fear which causes an undue protective spasm in the middle conscious. That is why so many fearful individuals have nightmares: their fears interfere with their natural communicative patterns with the soul. By fearing the messages that arrive in the mind, or their semblances, the middle conscious sparks a nightmare. For many of us, weird dreams are fun and quickly forgotten. For others, however, the dreams spark terrors that interfere with sleep patterns and cause even greater disruptions in the mental consciousness. Thus, once an ailment in consciousness is created, it is difficult to purge. Likewise, once false beliefs are widely instilled in a society, they are difficult to amend into truer beliefs.

The reverse situation is also true. For some of us, the sleep state is an exceptionally effective path to understanding more of the human consciousness. We can make use of our sleeping periods by learning more of the elements of our conscious minds which are being influenced by other levels of consciousness. Interpretation of dreams is very risky business, for dreams have no end of valid interpretations. Every element of every dream can potentially have infinite genuine levels of interpretation. A dream may be interpretive of a day's events, a recapitulation of several related experiences or precognitive of something about to happen. Or it could be all three and more. It may have elements of past lives that need to be resolved in the current life or there may be many communications from other souls to be processed by the integrated consciousness. The base soul processes most messages from other souls but some inevitably filter through to the mind in some form. Thus, many "divine inspirations" and visions arrive to those who seek them through sleep.

There is a great deal of value in asking for guidance from higher entities, even if you don't understand who or what they are. Even if you believe them to be some god or deity which should be worshipped, the mere asking for help and guidance is often enough to enlist the aid of some sympathetic higher soul. This soul will *not* be the ultimate Creator of the universe, or the single God of Christian and Judaic tradition or the Allah of Islamic tradition, or Buddha, Vishnu, Manitou or any other personified ideal. These other gods, as they have come to be known in the human world, are merely encapsulations of an idea, the idea that there are higher guiding forces and intelligences linked in a single universal way. This way, of course, is the way of life for all living beings — if life exists, certain common forces will result. On the soul's level of consciousness, one common trait is that there is a natural recognition of the forces of life and the integrated nature of evolutionary advancement. In other words, though we appear to be cut off from the lifeforms we call gods or mistake for gods, we really aren't. Our souls are in communion with them at all times, in various ways and through various levels of consciousness. Even though this book speaks of the base soul as a unified consciousness, it, too, has various subdivisions of consciousness. Like the mind, the base soul can function on the basis of constructive analysis or intuitive assimilation. It just happens to be far more adept at both.

Asking for higher guidance is often called prayer. The qualities of meditation and prayer are simply concentrations of consciousness, the focusing of the mind on a desired goal (even if the goal is transcending the mind). When the human being makes such an effort, he emits a portion of his consciousness into space: like all matter, the energy that produces consciousness radiates other energies which influence surrounding forces. When a signal of consciousness is emitted, it may be received by any other device or living entity which is compatible with it. Like a radio wave that is transmitted at a particular frequency, any compatible receiver within effective range can receive it. If such emissions of consciousness are deliberate, it is called "telepathy". The human being has two basic forms of telepathy: mental telepathy and soul telepathy. Direct communication between minds is subject for discussion in our world quite often, though some scientists doubt its existence. They prefer instead to discuss only the less effective but more discernible method of audible language, a form of telepathy in itself. It just happens to be audible frequencies instead of the exceptionally high frequencies of life. Soul communications, similar to mental telepathy, are the contacts established between souls. Thus, a soul may communicate with any other that receives its energy patterns. If a mind is trained to receive telepathically, it can do so, but most humans aren't trained for this at all.* Thus, a

---

*It is somewhat out of the scope of this book to enter a prolonged discussion of telepathy but it is certainly valid to say that there is such a thing. Furthermore, human telepathic ability is easily tested and statistical experiments have been used

The Cultivation of Man

prayer may be emitted by the mental consciousness and received by a compatible mind or soul. If the receiver is interested or capable of helping the individual who is praying for guidance, the subsequent action could well be noticeable.

If an individual who is under the impression he is praying to his god receives what he considers a desirable response, he will naturally reinforce his belief in that god. He may never recognize the true nature of the entity which did come to his aid. Like a simple shepherd seeing for the first time the wonders of modern electronic technology, any modern human from a technological society who encounters a consciousness from a higher world is bound to feel as though he has encountered a miracle. Yet if the people in our technological societies would begin to regard their historical religious beliefs in a more practical light (instead of hypothetically or superstitiously, as most do), greater contacts could be made. Although the human mind will never be a perfect telepathic instrument, its abilities can be enhanced. One way is through the traditional meditative practices taught by many mystics; another is simply by paying attention to your inner feelings and "voices".

---

for decades to measure this so-called psychic ability. To test your own ability, a simple experiment can be set up with the aid of a friend. The experiment consists of trying to project simple images into your friend's consciousness (and vice versa) and keeping score. The simplest method is to use the standard ESP cards used in parapsychological studies (five cards, each with a simple symbol). Shuffle the cards and try to project them to your partner who sits out of sight. About 200 trials should provide a statistically valid sample. With five different symbols, a score of 20 "hits" per hundred is chance. Significantly higher or lower scores indicate that there is either some telepathic ability being exhibited or some inhibiting factor. In parapsychological experiments, an exceptionally high score is 40 hits per hundred. In a personal attempt using this experiment, I noticed I was able to score slightly higher than chance. When I tried to enlist the aid of my guides through automatic writing, I scored 100 percent *wrong*, or misses. This astounding negative score I attribute to the principle that the learning process is a matter of individual effort; in other words, no effort to gain your own answers results in no help. Thus, the natural tendency of initiates to mystical communications to use the skill to predict the future or twist it to personal gain is usually frustrated. Our guides are not there to tell us the future, but to help us in the present.

Man's Unending Quest

Though human society has faced vast misery and violence because of beliefs which were sparked by higher entities, our basic feelings of conscience can be our saving grace. No human need bow to any entity or god he feels is bad for him. Though society often practices the vicious techniques of ostracization or corporal punishment to force those who stray from the path chosen by a dominant majority (or minority, in some cases), sooner or later humans must obey their own sense of rightness. Though we pray to idealized gods, we must see from the historical texts of religion, the Bible, Bhagavad Gita, Book of Mormon and other texts of supposedly "divine origin", that any god represented by these works is far from perfect.*

It seems that man's contacts with higher entities have often been based on the human beings cohering to the dictates and laws of a god. Those laws are to be followed and passed on to future generations on no other basis than they are given by something or someone who claims to be a Lord or other master of the human tribe he has contacted. The business of worshipping a god is taught unceasingly, the philosophy of giving to god taught nearly unceasingly. Why? How does a god use all this service? At best, we interpret this to mean that we should help gods by helping our fellow men and if we do this, something positive usually results. But often we simply follow the dictates of this teaching and force those who do question it to comply. The vengeful nature of many of our gods destroys their credibility as perfect beings, so why can we not just select from the ideas they pass on the ones we want? Humans seem too

---

*As I write this, I open the Book of Mormon at random, and glance down at this verse (Book of Alma, Chapter 9, Verse 24): "For behold, the promises of the Lord are extended to the Lamanites, but they are not unto you if ye transgress; for has not the Lord expressly promised and firmly decreed, that if ye will rebel against him that ye shall utterly be destroyed from off the face of the earth?" That form of interaction between man and higher guide, in my opinion, is far more harmful than helpful.

The Cultivation of Man

preoccupied with the notions presented to them by gods to ask themselves how much good those new ideas will do — and how much harm.

Any prayer that is answered by a higher entity may lead to two things: a) the answered prayer may help construct something worthwhile or b) it may tear down something worthwhile. Too often, humans merely follow laws and orders blindly, giving little or no thought to the effects of such obedience. Granted, rebellion can be a destructive and vicious thing, especially when anything gained by violence is usually held by violence. Yet it can also be a constructive force if it leads to a more just result: the violence usually enters when people disagree as to what is just. If we are taught a set of laws, say those of Moses, we have a tendency to defend them as absolutes, instead of mere guidelines. Laws, once set, become very inflexible and lose much of their response to individual circumstances. The laws given us by our higher guides are the principles by which they live. Though fine and valid and often relevant to human life, sometimes the relevancy is stretched a little thin. And sometimes, such as the commandment not to kill, impossible to follow. Thus, we twist and bend these commandments and laws to suit the order of the day. Thou shalt not kill means just that. But we interpret it to mean: "Thou shalt not kill your fellow man" or "Thou shalt only kill people who commit murder" or "Thou shalt only kill enemy soldiers". Each of these interpretations lessens the law and weakens it. When we find it enjoyable to eat meat, we presume it is justifiable to kill lesser animals. Yet it is wrong to kill anything, even plants. If we truly wanted to live within the bounds of the commandment, we would eat only carrion found by the wayside and plants which have died a natural end. Even then, microorganisms would be threatened and our very biological presence fills a portion of the biosystem that would push other life out. Thus, to survive, we must break the commandment. To justify ourselves, we simply define it to suit our own circumstances. It still provides a valid guide; we merely make it useful to us.

All the teachings of higher entities, particularly as reflected in our religions and guiding texts, are meant to help and guide men. Though the entities may have our best interests unquestionably at heart, they seem to succumb to the natural desire to be our saviors or rulers. Though much good comes from the relationship, the higher entities often seem to overstep the bounds of graciousness and use the controlling force of fear to enact their principles. Though the principles, once adopted, may set us upon a path to higher revelation and happiness, the techniques used to get us to accept them may be questionable indeed. The "fear of god" is often used (less so now than a century ago) like the threat of cudgel. Like the policeman who carries a nightstick as a visible warning to potential wrongdoers, the fear for the well-being of the soul after the death of the flesh is often used in human society to make individuals toe some political or religious line. To make the law even more imposing and impressive, a vast array of rituals are developed so that individuals know they are conforming to the expected norm. When the ritual becomes established, it too often becomes the focus of attention and the truth it was developed to serve is submerged. All our religious truths are submerged in ritual, like veins of gold in so much rock. Clouds of ritualistic claptrap follow every religion and virtually smother its founding purpose: the enhancement of human harmony.

The rituals of any society are the benchmarks of acceptance. If you conform to the basic principles and rituals of the society, you are basically accepted as a member of that society. Usually, the society devises a ritual of initiation to bring a child or young adult into the society. Baptism, the Bar Mitzvah, the ceremonies of various native peoples

The Cultivation of Man

all have the same purpose: to formally acknowledge a new member of society. The ritual itself means nothing. Marriage can be formalized as easily by jumping over a broomstick as by invoking the services of an institutionalized priesthood. The only relevancy is the factor of social acceptance: if the ritual is widely accepted, it is valid. Yet too often humans delude themselves into thinking or believing that there is some innate power in the ritual itself, as if splashing water on a baby's head or saying words over that water will change either the baby or the water. The only real changes effected thusly are those caused by societal reaction to the ritual. If the Baptism causes the child to be well received, the ritual was positive. If it causes him to be shunned, it was negative.

Ritualization is more of a universal trait than might first be imagined. All lifeforms which attain a certain level of intelligence find they must maintain some societal order for intercourse. The order is based on personal interaction, delineating the terms of reference for the actions and behavior of individuals within the social group. In primitive societies, social intercourse is based on the strong ruling the weak. Not only does the practice result from the ability of the strong to force the weak to do as willed by the strong, but becomes a part of the basic patterns of survival. Wolves, for example, have a very well-defined social order in the pack (see *Wolves of Minong*, by Durward L. Allen). The dominant animals breed together and get preferred treatment. When approached by subordinate animals, the dominant animal bristles, expecting to receive a gesture of submission. The gesture, as grandiose as the weaker animal rolling over onto its back to expose a vulnerable belly, is taken as due course. Rarely does a fight for supremacy result in death for either animal, if one of the lesser animals happens to vie for leadership. In the wolf pack, the social order extends from the top to the bottom, a pecking order established giving all animals in the pack a fixed social position. A fight between two lesser animals may not involve the dominant animals at all, though the dominant animal may interfere. A successful challenge on the part of a lesser animal is recognized by higher and lower animals in the pack alike, setting a new order.

The social orders of animals are founded in the principle of the survival of the fittest. As humans are basically animals like any other, our practices and rituals are just somewhat refined versions of the primal forces of social organization found in other mammalian species. Our codes of behavior may now be extended to include some that are not strictly oriented to the survival of the fittest but we can be certain they are founded in those very historical principles. The traditions of power structures and their associated rituals reach back to the dawn of our corporeal existence. They have resulted from what we are as animals; they have become as they are as much because of our corporeal structure as the forces of our consciousness. The rituals we practice are, of course, built into the daily activities and functions of human bodies. Our gestures of submission to a greater power, be it of man or supposed divine origin, are tailored to what we are. We bow or kneel rather than roll onto our backs or expose our throats. Yet the effect is the same and it stems from the same recognition: that to submit to a greater power is to avoid challenging it and therefore avoid the penalty of being vanquished.

Over time, tradition and circumstance change the interpretation of many gestures, their original meaning becoming either lost or submerged as the dictates of human society change. Whereas a gesture, say the courtly bow, may have arisen from the gesture of submission given a tribal chieftan, its intent now is far different. To the chieftan, the loyalty of his people, especially his warriors, is paramount. Without that loyalty, his survival as an individual, his success as a chief and perhaps the survival of the tribe itself would

The Cultivation of Man

be threatened. Thus, he must be assured of that loyalty. Like the dominant wolf, he may demand that his followers make gestures of loyalty and enforce the law with his own brute strength. Yet as his society evolves, as the tribal organization of the British Isles did, the social organization becomes more entrenched, stable and ritualized. If the social unit survives for a great length of time, its own history provides the impetus for much of its organization, creating and using rituals as forces of tradition recognized and respected by the people of the society simply on the basis that they are a part of that society. In the British Isles, as in many other cultures from Japan to Central America, this entrenchment resulted in the principle of the Absolute Monarch. The Absolute Monarch is accepted by the people as the individual with indisputable (though sometimes it is disputed) right to govern. In human tradition, this monarch is the one deemed to rule by the right of a god. His power supposedly comes from a god, either by being chosen directly or being the direct descendant of someone who was. The principle of divine right to rule has often become so entrenched in human society that it still refuses to die, even in countries which have chosen other forms of government.

In Britain, the Absolute Monarch eventually gave way to Parliamentary Democracy, which evolved its own tradition of Parliamentary Supremacy, which means Parliament can pass any law it wants. Yet vestiges of monarchy remain and Queen Elizabeth II and her family command tremendous respect throughout the world. Even in the U.S., where the British Crown was rejected in violent rebellion more than 200 years ago, Queen Elizabeth attracts the adulation of huge crowds whenever she visits the republic. The courtly bow is now granted enthusiastically to a monarch who holds no governmental power, merely the persuasive force of tradition and ritual. At best the bow may mean a gesture of loyalty to a country, ideal or tradition. At one time, however, a British monarch judged the depth of loyalty of his subjects by the depth of their bows.

Ritual is both disseminated and changed through time. The principles of British Parliamentary democracy, themselves evolved out of long monarchical tradition, and before that, tribal tradition, have been spread throughout the world. The U.S. constitution is founded on a variation of an earlier form of British Parliamentary democracy; Canada's founded on a later version tailored to overseas Dominions; and India's founded on a more modern version still. In each of these parliaments, the rituals and ceremonies are the outgrowth of first the historical relationships with founding peoples and second the localized practices indigenous to the individual country. The opening ceremonies of Congress in the U.S. have more than a hint of the opening ceremonies of Great Britain's House of Commons. And the British House of Commons still practices the ritual "barring of the doors", a ceremony born when an earlier Sergeant-at-Arms really had to bar the doors of the House of Commons against the forces of the British Crown. History sends out its tentacles in all directions, every event ever occurring having its vast historical context. The history of any simple ritual, practice or social ceremony can be born because of an event, such as the "barring of the doors", but still have its roots in the basic human need to survive. That need began long before any other ceremony known to man.

Ritual, with all its ceremonial garb and splendor, has apparently been a part of human society since at least the age of the so-called cave-bear cult of Neanderthalis. The expression of our inner desires and needs has always found itself in ritualized behavior. The mating dance of a prairie chicken is no less a structured social ritual than a blessing by the Pope. Both are means of achieving a desired end,

The Cultivation of Man

a practice seen or accepted as the natural way. Yet in human society, the biological needs of the organism are only part of the social structure: intellectual and spiritual needs also form a large part of our ritualized behavior. Though we often can't distinguish where the biological, intellectual and spiritual needs are separated, we can tell that there are distinct polarities. There is definitely a pattern established for the human mating cycle, a different pattern for the intellectual learning process and another for the pursuit of spiritual well-being. All three processes become wildly intermixed in the integrated social customs of any people: prayers are said in school; mating is sanctified by religious ceremony; and spiritual scholars seek religious truth through basic learning techniques. Our entire societies are geared to ritualized behavior. Table manners, courteous greetings and interpersonal respect are universal human attributes. All gestures, rituals and habits are formed on the basis of what the human being is, a bipedal organism in the atomical plane, but the need for ritual and social intercourse is more universal still. Each gesture, each formal ritual and each social habit is a contributing factor to social accord. Through this standardized behavior, individuals recognize consistency and are comfortable with their interactions with other members of their society. They provide a means of identification and interaction on a less conscious level. The individual does not have to waste valuable mental space studying the reactions of every encounter with other people to determine their intent if familiar gestures signal that intent. For example, if they carry the familiar gestures of friendship (smiling, holding out a hand for a handshake), you are reasonably certain you won't be attacked. Every gesture is based on the biological organism and what it can do: the handshake would never have been invented if we had no hands.

In evolving social organizations, the human animal has

developed a universal recognition of higher powers and intelligences that are not immediately apparent in this world. We are well aware of these forces through the highly ritualized teachings of our religions and social philosophies but have never actually studied the forces to determine their exact nature. Like other intelligent lifeforms, the higher entities that have contacted man in various ways demand certain courtesies to ease the interaction of divergent natures. Often, we have not understood the need for higher ceremony, only adopting the rituals and activities taught us by higher guides because we feared for our safety if we didn't. What we must understand is that higher entities, like us, must use structured ritual and systematic courtesies for social interaction. In higher worlds, where individuals can contact each other's consciousnesses far more easily and thoroughly than we can here, structured communication is even more important. Some of this knowledge has been passed on to us by our guides and much of it we have garbled considerably. Some we have even turned into the founding principles of new cults and religions. Yet overall, humanity has failed to understand the purpose behind his cultivation and focused instead on the flashier aspects of ritual. We even fight wars over how to practice certain rituals of worship, forgetting that to challenge the principle doctrine of worship is also our right.

Because of the simplicity of our forebears, we have evolved traditions of worshipping our higher mentors as gods, sometimes crediting them with powers beyond their reach. As discussed in Chapter 5, we have often confused our specific instructors with the general notion of a universal Creator. Although all lifeforms are related to this universal creative force, the notion does not supply much specific data for the definition of the human interrelationship with his planet. Rather than worship our guides (or gods, if you prefer), we would be vastly further ahead to respect them

The Cultivation of Man

as a son should respect his father. We should learn as much as we can from them but at the same time recognize how much the learning process can be disturbed by blind acceptance of dogma, whatever its origins. The rites passed on to us by higher entities most certainly had specific purposes at their first teaching. Yet these teachings are often bastardized through the ritualizations of various human societies. Just as British Parliament borrows notions of supremacy from an earlier governmental mode, so do religions borrow from their originating influences. Every Christian ritual, for example, is both the result of Christian influence and that of the earlier religious practices in the lands touched by Christianity.* Social indoctrination and ritual are not easily redirected and no historical tradition is dropped in an instant. It takes a very long time, hundreds and even thousands of years, for an entrenched practice to be erased from society. It may be changed or given new interpretations but it will maintain some presence. Thus, even Santa Claus has his origins in an earlier so-called pagan tradition. Though having very little to do with Christian origin other than to commemorate Christ's birth with gifts, it is now a very Christian tradition. Christian societies teach children to believe in Santa Claus the same way they teach them to believe in the Christian God. The only difference is that the misconception of Santa Claus is relatively short-lived. The misconceptions of the divinity are taught for the duration of the Christian's life.

Social training is the largest single factor in the prolongation of misconception. The ideas of the parents are passed on to the children and though they are systematically challenged in some way, and hence changed over a period

---

*For an interesting analysis of the rituals and practices evolving from the introduction of Christianity to the British Isles, read *From Ritual to Romance*, by Jesse L. Weston.

of generations, the core ideas usually remain intact. Thus, the massive social challenge of the Flower Children of the 1960s eventually cooled off to become a more conventional acceptance of the "Establishment" and a harmony with it. The erstwhile Flower Children found that to change society it was necessary to contribute to it; to contribute, they must conform. Thus, society changes, but it changes slowly and only when the forces of change become established enough to make themselves more powerful than the prior "Establishment". If massive social reorganization occurs too quickly, as it did during Stalin's first "Five-year Plan" and in Pol Pot's Kampuchea, the massive social cost is staggering. Social reorganization is better left to gradualists.

If we try to be better than our parents, we are exercising the basic human need to improve. To truly do justice to our concepts of liberty, justice and truth, we must allow every idea its right to be heard. We must forego the tools of brutality and unthinking indoctrination. Instead, we must teach our children to think for themselves, to question everything they encounter in life in search of a better way. If no reason can be found to justify an idea, why support it? Yet if an idea that is widely supported fails to be rationally supportable, we must beware erasing it: there are those who will jealously guard it. No notion of man, no matter how supportable it seems to be, has an indisputable right to govern. All ideas can be tested; none are as infallible as we would sometimes like to think. An idea has no more claim to perfection or divine right than any monarch or Pope: any and all are fallible.

Humanity may eventually learn that cherished notions are not absolute laws. No matter how much any society chooses to believe something, it must ultimately be prepared to lose that faith. There is always a greater truth to be known, a better perception and interpretation of truths already known. If an individual believes something because

The Cultivation of Man

his parents taught him to believe it, he must still test that belief. Though it may well be sound, it can undoubtedly be improved and better adapted to the conditions and circumstances of changing times. The force of change is universal. Just as we change, so must our ideas change. And as they change, so perhaps change the ideas of those higher guides who teach us. As we find better ways to learn, they may find better ways to teach. Human laws are not absolute. Nor are the laws taught us by higher entities. The only perfect laws are those of the universe itself, the perfect laws of nature.

But we can be certain that laws passed on to us through the vehicle of higher instruction are less imperfect than those devised by human warriors. To exist, society must be tolerant of change and learn to roll with the punches greater knowledge brings. At this point in human evolution, the static interpretation of gods and spiritual guidance is no longer adequate. We know enough about our environment and how it functions to identify what facts are possible within the context of the atomical world and what aren't. All that remains to be identified, therefore, are those facts which apply to realms outside the atomical. To do that, we must still avail ourselves of our higher guides. Thus, humans who reject religion need not reject the concept of higher guidance. They need only reject the fallacious ideas that surround religious truth. Our key to understanding is our rationality. That is our guiding strength in dealing with any foreign consciousness, our single ability to judge what is right and what is wrong. The blind acceptance of dogma and moral interpretation of the religiously devout cannot determine what is right; nor can the blind rejection of anything non-atomical. Moral right can only be interpreted from the heart of human endeavor. In that, we are our own guides.

8

THE MYSTIQUE OF MYSTICISM

There is much room in the modern world for the shadowy realm of human experience called mysticism. There is a mystique in the unexplained: it inspires belief. Though belief, as explained in the previous chapter, may be as much the result of social training as objective knowledge, most people accept some unproved beliefs as being true. Many of these beliefs center on religious or other mystical practices, an attempt by the human mind to reach out to some higher and greater power. In doing so, many humans become convinced that they can contact some such power and that the power will aid them in quests of their choice. As we shall see, such belief is not unfounded and often leads to a deep religious conviction. The nature of that conviction largely depends on the individual's frame of reference and societal history. If the individual is already a believer in some established religion or other metaphysical philosophy, he may deepen his belief or modify it to suit the new circumstances. Perhaps he will become "born again", as we often say of Christians who renew their faith. Or the experience may have the opposite effect, forcing the individual to drop some heretofore cherished belief. The realm of the religious experience is really no different than any other form of mysticism, the nature of the experience dictating the results. That prayers, studied meditation and other techniques of the mystic or devout do have significant effects is undeniable. We only doubt the supposed nature of these effects and seriously question the validity of "miracles" or "supernatural" phenomena witnessed by those who have opened themselves to mysterious powers. As a species, we tend to deal with our doubts through temporary denial, until the force of magnified truth presents itself to us in undeniable proportions. Even then, some of us reject obvious truths. Mysticism, in effect, is no more than a generalized term for the nonscientific exploration of unexplained effects. We can't know the root causes of all unexplained phenomena that have been manifested in this world but we can always search for them.

The human quest to explain mystical realities has led to many exciting questions and mysterious circumstances. We have created some very famous and wonderful cults of mysticism which seem to draw on unseen powers and have the temporal ability to enhance the powers of the human mind and body. As a discipline, mysticism provides the human being with some assurance of a higher organization of the universe as it relates to his life. The gathering of truth through meditation, yoga and other spiritual techniques is a reaching out of the human mind to some higher power that may in some way guide that human to a more satisfying life. The reaching out need not be in the context of an organized faith or religion, nor does there need to be a ritualized form of behavior. All that is required is the intrinsic human desire to improve.

Mysticism is a tool, just as science is a tool. The mysticisms developed by various human agencies throughout history have many common characteristics, mostly because they are based on a common element: the human being. Any religion, cult or stylized ritual is the result of a group of people attempting to standardize the effects discovered by the founder. As the ritualized practice spreads, it gathers

The Mystique of Mysticism

the momentum of historical tradition, whether it has any great validity or not. The actual mystic techniques on which the ritual is based, therefore, may be shared by many societies. Prayer, meditation and faith healing are three examples. Virtually every human society sooner or later stylizes these basic mystic practices into some form of organized social philosophy. The Asian mystic and the evangelical Christian have both discovered the same techniques; they merely express them differently in different social contexts. More, these techniques are accepted by most people in the world, whatever their background, and are used regularly.

In the quest for the greatest possible understanding, humanity has embarked on mystic rituals as a habitual path to social and personal evolution. Although mysticism has been part of the human experience since the human experience began, there is surprisingly little known about the forces which brought it into the human experience. For the most part, man accepts mysticism as part of everyday life, though usually a given social group will only accept its own localized practices. Whereas their own practices, however rightly or wrongly, are regarded as "truth", those of other social groups may be regarded as false, meaningless or even heretical. Yet mysticism is any practice that seeks to delve into the unknown without the benefit of the scientific method. Essentially, the difference between a mystic and a scientist who study, say, reincarnation is the methodology chosen. The scientist must first build a hypothesis which fits into what is already known by science and then carefully test that hypothesis until a theory emerges. Thus, empirical knowledge cannot step beyond the bounds of what can be proved by existing technology. The mystic, on the other hand, is free to experience his subject however he can. His proof is what he experiences, though the experience may not be freely replicated.

Man's Unending Quest

Having gained some knowledge of mystic phenomena or truth, the mystic cannot easily share this knowledge without transferring the experiential technique. His words fail him when he tries to explain to a novice how to astral project or meditate. The novice gleans only the barest awareness from his teacher and embarks himself on the trial and error process of learning the chosen technique. The scientist, whatever he may surmise, cannot accept any experience as fact in an empirical sense until it is reduced to quantifiable results. In short, he must translate it to numbers and mathematics. Failing that, the experience remains hypothetical. Yet in rejecting experiences that are not yet proved by the scientific method, the scientist shuts himself off from a wide range of experience.

For example, many scientists over the past few decades have denounced faith healing. This simple mystical technique is essentially based on many facets of the human consciousness but its intrinsic philosophy is that some higher entity aids in the healing process. Christians call this entity God. Yet the scientist ignores this primary element of the technique and instead discusses theories of "mind over matter", "power of positive thinking" and "power of suggestion". These vaguely defined ideas *seem* more scientific than they are. They do not explain the phenomenon but instead merely point out the way in which some answers may be found. Although vastly preferable to outright rejection of a very real element of human experience, the explanation remains inadequate. The human mind can indeed affect the health of the body for the better (as well as the worse) and so can the base soul. Yet what those elements of consciousness can do, so can other minds and souls. In fact, the same mechanical and biological processes which allow a person to use his own soul and mind to help cure himself allow others to come to his aid. If medical practitioners would become aware of this fact and exploit

The Mystique of Mysticism

it, they would be much more adept at curing many common ailments. More, the discovery of the hidden "gods" who aid in the healing process would also be hastened. The key to faith healing, as in all acts in life, is harmonious and beneficent cooperation. If a mystic (or any individual under any other title) discovers a way to exploit talents for healing via consciousness, he is as likely to be abused by his fellow man as used as an instrument of learning. His efforts to articulate his experience will necessitate the creation of new terminology which, in turn, will be subject to the vagaries of individual interpretation. What he knows so clearly and well is left for others to discover how they will. There is little he can do to pass on his technique.

The human failure to communicate effectively concerning mystical matters (indeed, concerning any matter) is as much the fault of undeveloped language as a failure to understand something new. Language is just too primitive to force all abstract concepts into speech. Thus, most of the human experience must be directly experienced before it can in any real way be accepted. The mathematical models of science are the only human means of truly translating abstract concepts of reality into abstract communications. In all other communication, the medium of direct experience is used as a foundation. Thus, to describe a fountain, common elements of experience (water, understanding of gravity) are used in presenting the idea of the fountain. Although the conceptualization is abstract, the model conceptualized is based entirely on the experiential. Unless the mathematical models of science are invoked, there is no empirical communication of the concept. Thus, a physicist is unable to truly describe a black hole in space or the conversion of mass into energy without relying on mathematical models. He is strained to equate such phenomena with phenomena more readily experienced by laymen. Unless the layman acquires the requisite mathematical training, his ability to understand a black hole is extremely limited.

Thus, the many humans who experience elements of the non-atomical are not able to pass on an understanding of the experience without creating an equivalent experience. Most mystical experiences cannot be replicated on demand and the very fact that most encounters with the mystical are accidental leaves the field of debate to the skeptic. Without hard, atomical proof, he will not accept the existence of anything non-atomical. Hence, each generation of skeptics rears another generation of skeptics to take its place. Those who do have mystical encounters can only continue in their own way to produce for themselves the startling effects they have discovered. And even though telepathy, for example, has been proved in scientific terms to be a statistically valid element of human consciousness, diehard skeptics insist the very idea is absurd. For the more enlightened who will view the evidence, the fact remains that explanations remain at bay.

Belief in an effect is shadowed by the unknown laws which govern that effect. If belief falls within a religious context, there is always the convenient "out" of the deity (or deities). For those who study metaphysics in a more secular sense, the answer simply remains a mystery. Whatever explanation is devised by either the religiously devout individual or the metaphysician, it will remain a hypothesis, for there is no possible way of testing it without the concentration of resources from a nonskeptical scientific community. And to date, the level of skepticism in the scientific community remains too high.

Despite the skepticism, the public interest in mysticism is as broad now as ever. Instead of the superstitious acceptance of some years ago, many unexplained phenomena are being considered very seriously. The unexplained, especially since the 1960s, has become a very

The Mystique of Mysticism

lucrative topic. People are prepared to pay a lot of money to have their questions answered, especially in areas that touch on the mystical. Books, T.V. and radio programs and all sorts of gurus have sliced their way into modern societies that are still seeking answers to ancient questions. People wonder more now than ever what the truth of God is, whether there is life after death and how much of the spiritual claims of Eastern mystics are true. Spirituality has become a commodity and the field is open to any entrepreneur. Though undoubtedly many people are living better because of the spiritual truths they have purchased from various T.V. evangelists and high-living gurus, the question remains: could they perhaps have learned the same truths with less cost? Fulfillment is very much a personal matter and the quest for truth leaves the balance sheet wide open in terms of value received. Essentially, if an answer you have devised (or acquired) fascinates and satisfies you, it is good. It need not work for anyone else. There is no single answer you can find and there is no single philosophy or way of life that is better than all others. All are only means of helping individuals find their way through life. If writing checks to your guru brings you pleasure, there are many gurus who take pleasure in receiving checks. Yet if discovering truth is your goal, you are well able to find any truth you seek at minimal cost. You have all the resources you need locked up inside you. Though it helps to have a guide, you needn't hire one: the most valuable guidance is free.

Yet even though there is much room for subjectivity in terms of spiritual truth, there are also absolute facts. For now, spiritual gurus and traditional religions prosper because science does not tread on their integral preserve: spirituality. Faith in abstract notions of god and the soul will continue as long as there is a scientific taboo concerning mysticism. Until mysticism is turned into an accepted field of inquiry, there will be little progress in broad human terms regarding spirituality. There are absolute laws governing the existence of gods and the soul and these absolutes can be discovered. Although science has determined that the stories of religion are essentially myths, it has done little to prove or disprove the mysticisms of religion. Religion (and therefore the substance of human history) is built around both myth and mysticism, myth being the stories told and mysticism being the actual practices, cause and effect relationships that touch other worlds and a whole new set of interacting laws.

Myths are easy to deal with. They interact with verifiable (or semi-verifiable) history: there is an archeological record which presents empirical data that can directly challenge a myth. The myth of divine Creation, for example, appears again and again throughout the world. Each time it appears, the archeological record can prove it false, *within the time frame set out in the myth.* Yet the stubborn recurrence of the basic myth points to a mystic force that inspires it in widely dispersed societies. Though the individual characterizations of the Creator and circumstances of Creation may vary greatly, it may only be this stylization that is wrong. The mere fact that so many humans have somehow devised the same basic myth strongly supports the underlying aura of mysticism: any human may be inspired in a similar manner.

The greatest mystery of human existence is the idea of higher life guiding the human species. The idea is central to all religion and mysticism, the efforts of which are usually to effect communications with such life. The methods used to make contact vary greatly but do work. When a person prays for guidance, he often believes his prayers are answered. A secular mystic may find techniques such as automatic writing help him communicate with a guide. Though skeptics will inevitably slough off every supposed instance of communication with higher entities as

The Mystique of Mysticism

"coincidence", the fact remains that such communications occur regularly. Otherwise, there would be no universal human effort to make such contacts. Each human being has his own guides (who may respond to a prayer in a manner consistent with the human's individual beliefs) and shares with them a unique relationship. These guides are built into the natural framework of this planet and no two humans have the same guides. The relationship between human and guide, therefore, is something intensely personal and is based, as many religions have long tried to tell us, on a special form of universal love and brotherhood. Communications are established between them as the human is capable (whether intellectually or otherwise) of receiving them. The base soul itself is aware of the higher guides but the mind must evolve a relationship on its own.

The principle of higher lifeforms involving themselves in our lives should not be construed as undue interference. Nor should anything we learn through such a relationship be accepted unquestioningly. Humans are often the recipients of higher learning and are expected to apply this learning in this world. Most recipients of higher teachings are impressed enough (whether or not they have any inkling of the source) to make profound realizations. They will therefore attempt to influence in some way their own lives, at least, and potentially widely disseminate the learning. That is how many organized philosophies and religions begin: an individual generates a new idea and others build on it until an organized structure, a bureaucracy, evolves. Though this certainly has been the case with such individuals as Christ, Mohammed and Buddha, any human being can be approached by a guide. Usually, the guide will select an individual for reasons known mostly to the guide but the human being may initiate contacts on his own. Contact can be initiated in many ways but, considering historical precedents, it seems prayer is one of the most likely avenues.

Man's Unending Quest

If a higher entity does contact one of us and leave with us a legacy of teaching, we need only study this teaching and learn from it. We need not enforce it, or take pains to build a church around it. As teachings spread, they deviate quite a bit from the original precepts and therefore there is no real purity of concept in this world. In the case of Christianity, Christ provided very worthwhile teachings that have been disseminated at the point of a sword for many centuries. From a weak and persecuted faith, Christianity has spread throughout the world, its first major breakthrough the acceptance of the faith by the Roman Caesars. At that point, the greatest teaching of Christ, the brotherhood of mankind, was disseminated by victorious legions that still haven't lowered their weapons. Only the faces and weapons change. The violence remains and through it the Christian faith has fragmented into countless denominations and sects. It is not the failings of Christ's teachings that Christians cannot live in brotherhood. It is the work of man's failure to heed and learn from the teaching. The work of this world is very definitely the work of man, despite contacts with higher guides.

We have learned much from our spiritual guides, though we do not understand much about them. We can learn more but we will learn most if we learn through the context of universal love. Through tolerance and open inquiry, the way should be paved for science to truly open its eyes to a discovery of the nature of human mysticism. There is little more to be gained from our religious quests, though many of us still use religion to provide spiritual succor. The mysticism of our past is currently our only window to the spiritual in any practical sense. We must raise that practicality to a level of empiricism that can make it an integrated part of our modern society. We will then know the meaning of religion and ritual and find more than succor in it: we will also find knowledge.

The Mystique of Mysticism

Western society is, perhaps, in the best position of any for an indepth exploration of the mystical. Enlightened scientific observation (as opposed to the messianic practices of some scientists) can provide much needed insight into the unexplained phenomena that so tweak the modern mind. We have developed a very advanced science in the Western world, though we have yet to build all the tools we need for a broader exploration of our environment. And despite our techniques, we still seem to demand a molecular base for everything, or at least a particle-oriented base. Though we have developed theories of such shadowy particles as the meson, neutrino and photon, we have yet to understand all of their principles. It will take many more years for technology to provide a clearer picture of the subatomic world; more years still before the extra-atomical is even begun to be explored methodically. Yet people still say (albeit less frequently) as they did in the 19th Century that man is on the verge of having discovered everything. Even though we know how limited we are corporeally, we still demand that the entire universe be explainable by the few basic human corporeal receptors.

We can't rely on our bodily receptors for a complete description of reality. At best, we can present to our minds rationalizations that work within our accepted societal framework. Societal training is a part of the human experience because as an organism the human creature must react in certain common ways to common experiences. There are very definite traits in any animal species and these traits are often translated into predictable behavior. The hunter who is most successful is the one who uses his knowledge of his quarry in the hunt. Societal training in the context of a cultured human society is really only an extension of our basic animal natures. We have learned certain characteristics that allow us to survive within our environment. One such characteristic is social cohesion. Our natural tendency is to identify with a sense of community, be it a neighborhood or nation. We learned this because it is to our advantage to form social units for mutual protection and benefit. As we evolve further from survival as a singular motivator, choosing instead comfort or amusements, we still exhibit our basic animal nature. Our creation of social clubs and team sports are a direct result of our natural desire to function as social units for mutual benefit. All the societal dressage that accompanies these creations merely illustrates our creativity, determination and the many other qualities that enrich our lives. We can't however, lose sight of the fact that the achievements of individual social units are the result of the use of common tools, primarily the human corporeal form.

The human body is a remarkable tool. It has many abilities that have scarcely been tapped. Our brain, that lumpish grey matter that captures so much of our scientific awareness, is merely a tool in itself, meaningless and worthless without a mind to drive it. It is the human mind, a structure based in energy, that creates intelligence and that is the core of our in-flesh awareness. This mind, for all its wondrous properties, is only an infant brother to the soul. What the mind may do and achieve is mirrored and magnified by what the soul can do. The two units are interlocking blocks in the human experience, both of which provide the human form with life, intelligence and self-direction. They are both the roots of all human mystical marvels, both in some way reponsible for all the magnificent mysteries that we can't yet understand. Although our corporeal organs capture most of our attention, for there is something in them immediately tangible to our senses, we would be nothing but lifeless atoms if we had no mind and soul.

We must learn that the perceptions of the body are not the absolute purveyors of reality that we like to think. We can only hope to refine our corporeal perceptions to the

The Mystique of Mysticism

point at which we can trust what they tell us. We can't escape, however, the fact that there is much beyond the range of those perceptions that will still somehow find its way into our minds. When that happens, we can't help but look beyond the pale of this world for an explanation of the mystery. We don't know how to look at realities that seemingly lie beyond our scope of perception, above our ability to understand. If we aren't taught to accept something, we reject it.

Our accepted reality depends entirely on the type of training we received as children. If we were trained to keep an open mind, we may find ourselves considering all sorts of impractical notions that prove in time to be fully plausible. Most of our most useful discoveries (the electric light bulb, the telephone, the airplane) have been the result of determined and visionary men who made their ultimate breakthrough in the face of vast societal doubt. These discoveries would still be awaiting discovery if the discoverers had accepted the standing societal notions that something or other is impossible. The prime ingredient of success for these discoverers was their perseverence, their prime motivator their determination and their prime skill their ability to look at truth differently than the general populace. To prove their theories, to discover their truths, they first had to reject much of their societal training and orient themselves to a new perspective. To prove themselves correct, they first had to prove many others wrong. Yet think of the false notions man has stripped away: the earth's surface is not flat; the sun does not travel across the sky over a stationary earth; heavier-than-air machines can indeed fly. The human mind can reorganize itself to accept greater truths: it need only make the effort. If the mind fails to adjust to discovered realities, it only deludes itself. For who can still seriously argue that the earth is flat?

As a species, we are forced to define our truth in terms

of our own beliefs. As most of our beliefs are taught as we grow through childhood, we are often subjected to mountains of ill-perceived claptrap that only hampers our interpretation of truth. Think of all the racial slurs that are cast about the world, yet it should be obvious to all that there are really very few elements of human nature that differ from race to race. For the most part, a human being is a human being, despite localized behavior patterns. Our essential motivators are the same, our essential reactions to environment are the same. Thus, cultural differences are the result primarily of social training, the indoctrination of individuals to behave in harmony with the mainstream. Once a belief is taught, all other beliefs must vie with it for a compatible place. If no such place can be found, a mental blockade emerges: the two beliefs confront each other and perhaps force the mind to take measures of self-protection. Thus, two beliefs that seem incompatible may force the rejection of one or the other, though both may hold equal truth. Only the context of belief as instilled through social training allows selection of one or the other.

Once beliefs have been instilled, they die hard. In the rebellion of youth, many people try to reject the teachings of their parents but few do more than modify those teachings slightly. There is no way to completely reject any teaching, to remove its stain from your life. You may act contrary to the teaching, you may even purge it from your immediate consciousness but its influence will remain. Your only guide in resolving the many conflicting teachings presented to you in the course of your life is your logic, reason and wisdom. Using those innate tools, you may be your own best judge of truth and thus base your decisions and actions on your own truth. If you study the vast array of teachings handed by man down to man, you will see that no two are truly compatible. At best, they do not contradict each other; at worst, they deny each other's existence. Yet many beliefs

The Mystique of Mysticism

have common truths, some of which may earn your trust and thus provide the core of your personal belief structure.

Whatever your beliefs, you must realize that they are not complete. At best, you have a fundamental grasp of the major elements of your immediate existence. You still know little of the forces beyond the immediate atomical realm. You must reside as an earth-bound entity who interprets his environment through barriers of perception. You must, therefore, accept much of your circumstances on faith: that life and material reality are as you perceive them, or at least similar. You must have faith that the moral principles and values you use to guide your actions have relevance and validity. Whatever the notions you hold about the ultimate structure of the universe, it is only your faith in your own perceptions that allows you to maintain intellectual equilibrium. If your perceptions, beliefs and intrinsic interpretations of reality are too greatly challenged, you may slide into insanity.

Your mind, or more specifically, your rationalization, is the focal point of your earthly existence. If rationality should capsize under stress, your greatest tool for self-direction within this plane is lost. Until you regain control of your mental faculties, the guidance of the base soul is lost or, worse yet, misconstrued and twisted. Thus, the motivation for maintaining firm beliefs is strong. The mind's natural tendency is to impart as much faith as it can in its beliefs and is reluctant to risk altering them too drastically. Thus, the human devotion to ideals sometimes outstrips the rationality the ideals are meant to strengthen. Ideals are often held like a charging battalion's banner, an inviolate icon to be protected to the death. Yet the reality of the mind is that it is not inviolate and that ideals do change. In spite of a human tendency to become slaves to ideals, ideals can and should be periodically tested. Only then can they be accepted with reasonable conviction. As time goes by, the circumstances around an ideal change and therefore the perceptions of that ideal change. In terms of mysticism, which has promulgated most of the world's primary ideals through religion and its offspring, politics, a few basic ideas have served man for all of man's history. Yet the current tests of science are more rigorous than anything they have ever encountered before and only the bare-bones abstract philosophies seem to be surviving. Though man has traditionally impressed his children into following given religious or political philosophies, society as a whole is challenging ideas once accepted blindly and rejecting many of them.

In effect, religion is the historically dominant philosophic force and its dominance is based on impressment. The root of the impressment is the profound influence a few guides have been able to gain over their human counterparts. These entities, whatever their basic motivations for contacting the human world, have often found it more expedient to gain control over humans through the human sense of fear than through a rational approach. The force is obviously still at work as new cults spring into existence demanding the unquestioning loyalty of their followers. On an individual basis, the contact by an entity from another plane opens a door of practical rationalization that had always been safely abstract. The individual must resolve the practical appearance in his world of something he never really had to test before. It is one thing to believe in God and another to confront something god-like. And when that god-like presence uses its impressive initiative, the faltering and fearful human being will believe almost anything.

The key to mysticism will be the breaking down of this great unknown. As humans lay down their loyalties to their various gods or philosophical convictions, they are making rational decisions based on fear, trust, incessant training and everything else they have ever encountered in life. If an

The Mystique of Mysticism

individual is "god-fearing", he is iconizing an idea of a divinity that doesn't exist as he pictures it, yet the existence in his own mind is real. His conceptualization of the deity is based on what he was taught it could be or should be but is fundamentally misdirected. If we really want to resolve the great unknowns of human existence, we have to be prepared to reject our personal notions in favor of the truth. Undoubtedly, there are many cases in which a higher entity has deliberately instilled misdirected notions in responsive humans which have influenced human history. Humanity still struggles with vestiges of this social training. We have been taught for so long to believe in deities without trying to understand them that no one to my knowledge has ever seriously tried to measure any energy that may emanate from a godly source. It is almost as if we are afraid of what we may find.

True enough, taboos still linger in the heightened intellectual activity of the modern world. Though the mass of educated people in the world find it increasingly difficult to rationalize the existence of gods as depicted in religions, they seem reluctant to let go of the idea altogether.* We seem divided in two camps: a) that there are deities as depicted in religions or b) that there are no deities. We apparently reject or fail to consider any half-way point: can there not be entities of a higher nature than us, which are not necessarily stylized gods? Any realistic study of human philosophy will eventually lead to such a position, providing the trained biases of the individual do not interfere too radically with rational thought. Logic, not religious teaching, is our guide through our search for truth: too few of us realize that.

---

*Periodic Gallup public opinion polls in the U.S. indicate that acceptance of certain traditional Christian beliefs such as Heaven and Hell is slightly lower among those Americans with college level education than those with high school or grade school education. See *Adventures in Immortality*, by George Gallup, Jr. (see reading list).

Historically, religious teaching has focused on mythology more than truth. While mythology presents some worthwhile precepts and illustrates morals, it is also bizarre. Myth is not necessarily completely false: it merely extends the hope of some ingrown truth. Defining that truth, however, is chancy. Unwisely, too many people perpetualize myths to justify doctrine. While myths of several cultures may have great similarities even when the cultures do not, the myths alone do not present the truth. They only represent truth in the abstract, carrying with them all the embellishments of active imaginations. For instance, four basic myths that recur throughout the world seem to delineate a common human perception of human existence. These are: the Creation myth, the deity (or deities) myth, the life-after-death myth and the reincarnation myth. These four myths can be used to construct a composite of primitive human understanding of how the human fits into his universe.

This composite can be briefly characterized as the creation of the universe by an intelligent force which did so out of personal interest or loneliness. At first, the sky was created and populated with many kinds of lifeform, some animal-like and others spirit- or demon-like. The earth was then created and at first, the animals and spirits of the earth cooperated and lived happily with the sky spirits. The Supreme Entity allowed nature to take its course until a man was placed upon the earth. This man was the founder of the people (i.e., the relevant tribe). He was a good man and also cooperated and lived happily with both the lifeforms of the earth and the sky until some malevolent being arrived. After vanquishing the malevolent being with the aid of helpful spirits and the Supreme Entity, the man died and went to live in the sky with the sky spirits and the Supreme Entity. Life there was happy and idyllic and lasted forever. Ever since, the people have tried to earn their way into that

The Mystique of Mysticism

place of happiness by improving themselves over many incarnations.

Interestingly, this composite varies little from either the myths of the Yanomami of the Brazilian rain forest, just exposed to white civilization this past century, or with the older Creation myth of Genesis. The idea, although vastly more widespread than any devised by archeologists, is obviously not supported by science. Why, then, does it keep recurring? Our imaginations may be the tools that flesh out the skeleton of the story but the skeleton seems absolute. The concept of human creation by an intelligent force is nearly universal and the concept that the human soul survives the corporeal flesh more so. Meanwhile, books are added to books which describe the mystical near-death experiences of thousands of people. Others deliberately seek out mystical encounters and often publish their experiences. The similarities of mythology and the case histories of both accidental and deliberate encounters with the unknown are astounding. Yet still science wavers in its quest: these thousands of years of cumulating data should have wrought some theory acceptable to science. Yet science shies away from even hypotheses. Man still struggles with the definition of his atomical world, so seemingly solid yet so microscopically divisible. And though for thousands of years his guides and highest teachers have given him the formulae he needs to discover the truths of his own self and his origins, he fails to do so.

Man must use the wisdom of his old myths and his mystic techniques to lead him into himself. If we marvel at a mystic's ability to tread on hot coals or to touch some higher form of consciousness, we need only realize that he is a human using human tools. Whatever he does, anyone else may do, should he train himself for the task. But if the feat is never accepted as having been done, it may never be repeated. The challenge of the modern world is not to expose all mysticism as a sham but to find the definible base for what really does happen. Whereas an earlier age could be content to let the unexplained rest on a deity's shoulders, modern man has no such comfort. He knows too much to allow such an attitude to continue: as he learns more, such archaic attitudes, including the blind denial of skeptics, will become ever more hard pressed. The time for a scientific expansion into the world of the mystic is at hand — the result will be an emerging Science of Metaphysics.

9

THE SCIENCE OF METAPHYSICS

At this point in its evolution, the Science of Metaphysics is more than just a philosophy but remains an unformed discipline that has no established academic base. In effect, it is in much the same position as psychology at the turn of the century or chemistry 300 years ago.

The organization of any discipline takes time. Human thought must always evolve to the point where it is possible to accept a new discipline. All the academic disciplines taught in our universities and schools, for instance, are the result of long struggles on the part of pioneering individuals who believed truth to be worth the risk of challenging established thought. The body of knowledge man has gathered through the ages has been won at the price of much blood and hardship. Yet it has been amassed and is focused to a large extent in our formal educational institutions. Many of these institutions are like pinpoints on the frontiers of knowledge, providing a buffer between the known and the unknown, developing theory to find fact. As fragments of knowledge are considered, compared and compressed into a working theory, the academe stands by like a volatile judge. No new knowledge comes to have lasting effect, it seems, if it is not in some way incorporated into the academic curricula of the world: we study what interests us. Nor is new knowledge accepted without rigorous challenge, as new knowledge invariably presents contradictions and anomalies in the face of the established body of thought. To force a new discipline into academic acceptance requires a great deal of concentrated effort, yet it is done.

Formal education is really a product of the wish or desire to give people the best of currently available knowledge. For all their weaknesses and vacillations from one pop curriculum to the next, the world's educational processes are showing a marked expansion as learning devices. As human awareness of the human condition expands, there come greater demands on the current body of knowledge and greater demands on those who seek to disseminate it. There are also many demands of a moral nature: whereas it is easy enough to present knowledge to young minds, it is far more difficult to teach them to use it wisely. Thus, to incorporate new disciplines into the educational system means accepting inevitable challenges. If the disciplines eventually prove worthy, they are accepted. Perhaps the greatest challenge facing any new discipline is that of satisfying some basic human need to know.

Chemistry, for example, forced its way into the accepted realm of formal education because it answers some very basic questions about our atomical environment. In essence, chemistry, joined with the other physical sciences, *is* the study of our atomical environment. Although other elemental realities do enter the picture, our perception of any truth beyond atomical reality is hopelessly shadowed by our current limitations. We can't easily determine the nature of realities that are totally foreign to our experience: we can only relate to them within the context of that which we already know. Chemistry, as a discipline that explains the natural relationships of chemical actions, tells us a great deal about the *configuration* of our world. When we consider these configurations in the light of, say, the relationships we ascribe to the discipline of physics, we

The Science of Metaphysics

emerge with a pretty good idea of how our atomical world functions. Biology, sociology, psychology and many other disciplines evolved as the result of our efforts at finetuning our understanding of our existence. Although a discipline such as economics does not lend immediate comparisons to atomical theory, its roots can be traced to such basic experiences as the heft and size of cargo in a ship's hold which contributes to a country's gross national product. As we come to understand our environment better, we realize that all of our disciplines are simply fragmentations of a whole; we fragment our experience for the purposes of analysis, then try to put the picture back together in the light of our new understanding.

New understanding often means letting go of the old. As the early alchemists once thought, it is indeed possible to turn lead into gold. Their efforts, although failing in their stated purpose, did lead to the development of chemistry. Further, advancements in chemistry led to the development of nuclear physics. Nuclear physics in turn proved that through fission and fusion, atomical elements can be reconstructed: lead can indeed be turned into gold, though at great cost. Although the alchemists were wrong in believing they could find a base substance that would perform the Midas touch, their basic idea of transforming elements was not. The alchemists were misguided by the infancy of their science and many scientists have been more wrong. In our quest for truth, we must always beware of "a little knowledge". What seems possible today may prove impossible tomorrow and vice versa. Like the second-year university student, man has often been very certain of his answers. Yet time has a way of mellowing both the student and ideas: there is little likelihood that any interpretation of facts will ever be exactly correct. Interpretations are too open to change as perspectives broaden and knowledge deepens.

Man's Unending Quest

When we enter the realm of determinist thought, which is essentially that all things have their causes, we find it all too easy to make summary judgements. Causal relationships, however, are never as simple as first investigation makes them appear. Although the Karmic truth that for every action there is an equal and opposite reaction is absolutely true, sorting out which causes result in which actions is often a task of monumental proportions. Although it is easy to reach into a history text, for example, and come up with a handy slogan that seems to summarize the reasons why a nation went to war, the actual circumstances of the time were never that simple. Inevitably, the serious scholar of history finds that tracing the root causes of any event leads him hopelessly far afield. In the end, he must base his theories on assessments of causal relationships in a relative state. Each cause must be measured against all other perceived causes, such as the political, social, economic and human elements that could have had significant effects. If war was declared, what were the predominant philosophies of either side? Who opposed the war? What would be gained or lost by armed conflict? Who were the decision-makers and what were their immediate influences? What were their historical and childhood influences? The possible factors are infinite, yet many are more relevant than others. Weighting each one for its appropriate degree of influence is the trick. What war was ever truly fought because of a slogan?

Yet science itself is the deterministic search for causes. There is no more determined individual than he who devotes his life to the exploration of a cause. To find an answer is to challenge any other answer that differs. To survive such a challenge, the new answer must endure much conflict. There is no easy way to bring knowledge before the masses of humanity and explore the unknown without challenging the very foundations of all that is already known.

The Science of Metaphysics

To a large extent, our perception of the world is simply interpretation. If we ever develop our inherent abilities to perceive beyond the atomical to the point we are capable of, we will see how wrong many of our firm impressions are. We will find, for instance, that the sun not only warms our earth, but also provides base energy for all the planes of this planet. That energy provides base matter shaped by many lifeforms that have no direct association with our plane. Though there are still many things to question in our own world, it is now time to turn our minds to another frontier, one that has been with us as long as we have had the most elemental awareness.

The question of metaphysical thought being transformed into a heightened science goes beyond mere explanation of misunderstood phenomena. It will provide the basis for understanding the worlds beyond our known atomical world. Just as psychology has begun to open the mind to new and effective means of exploration, so will metaphysics open the realms of the soul. Even as psychology was an unpopular discipline with established academia in its early days, it has since gained repute. Psychology as the study of the human mind is still in its infancy but it has progressed to the point where established schools of thought are freely hammering out theories about intelligence and self-direction. For the most part, the theories are crude and at times quite naive but the direction of the discipline is taking form. It is taking form so well, in fact, that it is beginning to shut itself off from certain avenues, and doing so within the branches of the discipline as well. For instance, psychologists rarely speak of the soul, preferring to treat the concept with disdain. Yet at the same time, they try desperately to concoct a term that means the same thing and have so far failed. Their efforts are polarized, with behavioral psychologists looking for roots of behavioral training for all human activity, physiological psychologists trying to discover the mind in the electro-chemical reactions of the brain and analytical psychologists tampering with the errant behavior of individuals. None of these branches reaches to the core of the human being; they do not touch the true depth of the self, the soul and all its attendant characteristics. Until they do, psychology remains an unformed discipline.

The nature of the human soul is such that it is largely invisible to the human senses. That it is there is obvious because we carry life. Somehow we live and there can be no doubt that there is something basically different in the way the human form is composed and, say, the way a crystalline rock is formed. Our experience carries intelligence and self-direction. We are motivated by our own goals, which a rock is not capable of forming. The rock simply exists; we progress. We are living entities and are therefore responsible for our lives, whatever we do with them and however we choose to perceive them. For the most part, we are willing to transcend such consideration of purpose and merely attempt to achieve our goals. Individually, we may have trouble in establishing a worthwhile life-goal but nonetheless our purpose awaits us. If we were simply the products of electro-chemical impulse, we would be as lifeless as rocks. Life, if it emanated solely from the corporeal, biological organism, would be as ephemeral as each human incarnation and far less directed by experience and instinct. There would be no innate wisdom, no base of experience which the soul provides. Even as beasts of the forest, which we would never rise above, we would be ineffective, because we would have no instinct. All these qualities are drawn from our past lives, where experiences are translated into the actual matter of our base souls. If we had no divisible soul, we would have no mythologies of death, only a grim forebearance. Even though the proof of death is known only truly to those who die, there are millions of humans who were revived from the brink of death (many of whom were

The Science of Metaphysics

clinically dead) and described remarkably similar experiences afterwards.* Though their bodies were on the verge of death, their consciousnesses remained alive and continued gathering experience. That is how the soul survives: it adapts to each changing reality, including death.

We can't be certain of all the influences of the soul on the course of a human life, for as described earlier, the soul is often subdued beneath the mind which provides its own motivations to a significant degree. More, the mind interprets the soul's basic motivations, reacting to them in keeping with societal convention and its own incarnate experience. Without the guidance of the soul, the mind would have no sense of purpose, yet it may still not direct its energies entirely to the soul's favor. Only by discovering the exact relationships of mind, soul and body can modern man come to an acceptable understanding of the human being. As we categorize and mechanically measure the varied energies which make up the human consciousness, as we have classified our atomical environment, we will have the means of guiding our human destiny to its fullest potential. If we did not detail our experience in taxonomic models, we would still be like the deer in the meadow, grazing contentedly, fearing only death.

The human mind is the result of a complex evolutionary process that began with the creation of the universe. The nature of that Creation may always remain a mystery but there is much to be gained by tracing history farther and farther into the past. As we learn more of our past, we are able to apply that knowledge to the improvement of our lives. For instance, the development of Darwinist theory allows us to see more clearly how the human being relates

---

*According to a Gallup poll (1980/81), as many as 23 million Americans have had a "verge-of-death" or "near-death" experience, of which as many as 8 million have had some form of "mystical" experience along with it. *Adventures in Immortality*, by George Gallup, Jr., Page 6.

to his environment. As a product of that environment, his knowledge of the interrelationship will obviously aid him in living longer and better. Although there are still Christian Creationists and other fundamentalists who dispute Darwinism, they have no substantiable evidence to support their contradictory claims. The fossil record clearly indicates that biological species evolve systematically in response to environment. In the case of the human being, that evolution has been systematically upwards in terms of intelligence. Yet the fossil record does not show how intelligence came to be but merely maps the steps along the way. Thus, there are major gaps in our knowledge of our own evolution and therefore in our understanding of our place in our environment.

To understand *what* has happened, however, helps us to understand *how* and *why*. When we find that old theories leave us grasping with empty hands, we turn to new disciplines. We have found motivation for change in environment, the physical need to survive the greatest. Yet we don't understand *how* the motivation for survival led us in this particular direction or *why*. Gravity will bend our bodies, the sun will form genetic codes that govern skin pigmentation and time will certainly lead us to death. These factors are simply physical motivators, causes of effects where neither cause nor effect is based on intelligence. The effects are as purely physical as a rock falling off a mountainside. But in addition to that, intelligence can affect the shape of our bodies and the length of our lives. Machines help us build things, live longer and see better. We can organize ourselves as more effective social units, decide to stop smoking and take fewer risks when driving. These decisions are based on intelligence, which sees self-interest as its motivator. Yet still we don't understand that intelligence. Although we have become as we are, we don't really know how or why.

The Science of Metaphysics

Even as we begin to master our own intelligence and gain control over our destinies, we fail to understand why one man becomes a carpenter and another a musician. We only know that the personal choices are the result of the individual personna, the product of desires and wishes that each of us tries to fulfill. We all choose our station in life and seek to build on that. Our contributions may be great or small but they remain ours. As we are all irrevocably bound to environment and are products of environment, we must realize that all of our desires and wishes also stem from environment and will be expressed through environment. That, too, is the purpose of life and Humanity's specific purpose is to improve itself the only way it can: through environment. Thus, every experience we have, even if we enclose it totally in our minds, is the product of everything experienced externally.

Many people say that such skills as telepathy, communication with the souls of the Afterlife and contacts with higher entities are impossible. Having no immediate experience (i.e., none recalled by the mind) of such occurrences, it is perhaps easy for them to maintain their beliefs. For those of us who have experienced these phenomena directly, there is no doubt that they are real. The only question concerns the mechanics and motivations of the contacts. Whereas the "what" is fully apparent, the "hows" and "whys" remain at bay. The mechanics are not so far-fetched for the imagination to grasp. Even simple auditory communications are a form of telepathy, a low-frequency communication that requires the interface of an atomically based neurological system and a mind. It is the mind, a non-atomical structure, that interprets these communications. When it thinks, the mind is operating at a higher frequency than can be conveyed through human voice. It is not unreasonable, therefore, to consider the act of communicating from mind to mind as possible. In fact it occurs all the time, with little thought given to the occurrences. Any intelligence capable of driving the human body to effect speech in its many configurations may also learn to circumvent that speech, even if only momentarily.

Holistic thought is summing up all thoughts in an instant. This flash of understanding is the mechanism used by the soul and, less effectively, by the mind when they circumvent the body. The body, though there to be used, is simply not used for that action. The chosen task is completed without the body because, for that task, the body is not required: experience is gained through different environmental means. As in-flesh entities, we cannot circumvent our bodies for any great duration, for the consciousness remains physically joined to the body. Although the mind may travel widely through astral projection, the soul remains joined with the body until death. Because of this physical joining, both the soul and mind may evolve and grow: new experiences can be physically "stamped" into the fabric of consciousness. It is the body which makes that physical memorization possible. Otherwise, we could spend ages in learning but never really have the ability to permanently implant the memories gained. When the soul joins a higher plane, it must join a new form of body, using the astral matter of that plane for its evolutionary growth. That, essentially, is the distinction between the Afterlife, which is a place of rest for souls, and the higher planes where dwell our higher mentors. In the Afterlife, growth is limited, although experience is freely had. In the higher planes, as in the atomical plane, there is nonliving matter that can be assimilated into the actual matter of living beings. Even as we depend on our corporeal bodies for nourishment of the mind and soul, so do they. It is only the energy matter that differs, and even that may be traced to a common source. Thus, it matters little whether an individual human being believes in the Buddhist Nirvana

The Science of Metaphysics

or the Christian Heaven. Both terms apply to a place of growth, where the spirituality of the soul, a concept we treat so abstractly here, is a matter of physical survival. The soul, like the body, must eat. It merely chooses different food.

Metaphysics, therefore, is not a window to the supernatural or the wildly abstract. It is simply another discipline that will open a new vista of discovery for human eyes. Given its dictionary definition, metaphysics is the study of the nature of being. In essence, that includes the entire universe. More specifically, however, for we must always narrow our focus when studying something, metaphysics is the study of the soul. Although there is no such thing as the supernatural or magic, there is certainly much that exists outside the realm of the atomical. Metaphysics, having historically dealt with the tapping of higher forms of consciousness through the intellect, paves the way for a more organized study of the soul. Although the specialization of the field will inevitably force upon it biases, as all sciences force upon their followers, man has no other recourse for learning of the soul. His philosophical disciplines have taken him as far as they can: what he needs are verifiable facts. Only then can the soul step from behind the smokescreen so ubiquitously laid by scientists and clergy alike.

The specialization of any discipline is fraught with pitfalls. It is a paradox that the most advanced tools of knowledge used by man are also so severely handicapped by their own specialization. Any specialist, by the very nature of being a specialist, drives himself into a corner in which he can only see the ever-narrowing specialty he studies. He chooses a small fragment of a fragment, which in turn sees little more than itself. If a psychologist, he studies first and foremost the human mind; if a behavioral psychologist, he seeks to prove how the mind is trained through environmental influence to behave. He neglects the broader spectrum of consciousness which allows that mind to behave:

the soul. The analytical psychologist, however, knows there are deeper mysteries to consciousness than the immediate experiences of the individual. But can he convince his colleague?

There is a vast body of knowledge which can be applied to the metaphysics of the soul. There are the decades of laboratory work in psychic phenomena, which have proved telepathy, clairvoyance and psychokinesis to be real. There are thousands of case studies of precognition, memories of past lives, near-death phenomena and unexplained apparitions. Many people train themselves in the simple technique of seeing and identifying the colors of the human aura, the radiation of life-energy from the human Spirit. If the skeptic cares to challenge his skepticism, there are thousands of volumes of published material that all point in the same general direction, no matter how widely varied their context: that there is a human soul. Why, then, does modern society fight the concept and not plunge into a hearty quest to understand the soul? The challenge is there, the technology can be developed and the theory laid out in this book provides a sound framework. If the information contained in these pages is pursued, the discovery of the soul is not so far away. For the most part, the book consolidates what is already known. The new information is the gift of higher awarenesses man has always called gods. Perhaps it is time we all learned to call them guides.

APPENDIX

Automatic writing is a skill. Like any other skill, it must be learned. True, it helps to have a natural facility, just as it helps to have a natural facility for painting, accounting or skateboarding, if those are the skills you choose to learn.

Automatic writing is also a form of communication. Like any other form of communication, it takes two. In other words, even if you prepare yourself for the task (I'll explain how in a moment), you will still have to find someone to communicate with. The souls of other worlds have many and varied interests, only one of which is communicating with in-flesh humans. More, as many books dealing with automatic writing warn, there are disturbed and playful souls that may be contacted by the little-prepared human. You must be prepared to be frightened or at least tricked: automatic writing is not a Saturday evening parlor game.

For many, no amount of endeavor will make automatic writing work. The barriers an individual can set up in his mind against accepting something contrary to what his society has trained him to accept are incredible. More, many people will just not have the interest or ability to orient their minds to an acceptance of automatic writing. Some people want desperately to do automatic writing, as others want desperately to be Hollywood actresses, yet not have the drive or determination to succeed. In other words, if you are not willing to accept the sacrifice of time to make it work, you will not likely succeed.

But for those of you who are willing to try sincerely, there are great rewards. There are also dangers, but these can be minimized by one simple realization: no soul can hurt you except through your willingness to hurt yourself. Therefore, if you are communicating with some intelligence other than your familiar mind and friends, let your wisdom be your guide. If you are asked or commanded to do something outrageous or harmful, ignore it. There is no use in upsetting your life to gain truths that you may learn more easily in another context. Keep in mind always that you are the ultimate master of your destiny. Worship who or what you want but there is no divine force (or evil force, for that matter) which will punish you for not accepting something you are taught through automatic writing.

So, you are ready to begin. You have been informed, instructed and warned. All you need now is a pen and paper, either of which may be of any form you are comfortable with. Although not a requisite, it is desirable to practice automatic writing in private. For the most part, you will be more comfortable in private and you will have more control over the experience. Interruptions should be avoided, as you will want to concentrate on what is happening. A ringing telephone or demanding children are not conducive to a carefully engineered learning experience. In fact, you may wish to select a time of day which you may use consistently and privately. The place may be anywhere you are comfortable but souls do have a decided preference for older houses with high ceilings. I don't really know why. Even so, low ceilings should not impede the process.

When you first sit down to a session of automatic writing, you should clear your mind of your daily troubles and relax. You need not attempt transcendental meditation

Appendix

or to put yourself into a trance. Many natural psychics will fall into a trance-state quite beyond their control. This can be extremely distressing and if it happens to you as you write, proceed according to your daring. At any rate, the technique consists of touching the pen lightly to the paper and forming a question in your mind. If you speak the question, it will certainly be projected from your mind at the same time, which is how you communicate with the other side. They will communicate in like form, sending thought impulses to your mind. You may recognize words forming in your mind as the pen begins to move. Try not to let your mind start shaping the words; that is, do not direct the conversation. The pen should move of its own volition. You do not have to move it. If you do, you are not using automatic writing but playing a charade.

At first, the pen may move rather shakily. That is how it began for me. Yet I don't doubt that some people will begin with strong, deft strokes right off. It seems many people have a natural psychic ability and the words run through their fingers like quicksilver. For myself, the technique required a little practice. After a few weeks, however, I was able to proceed quite smoothly. Eventually I graduated to the typewriter.

As the writing progresses, you will find yourself leaping excitedly from one topic to another, seeking answers to all the great questions of your life. Do not be surprised if the answers are cryptic and contain little information. The guide's task is to *guide*, not provide facts and information. Do not try to guess your future, which at first is a strong temptation. If you do, you may be unlucky enough to find out. More likely, however, you will be fed some misleading stuff that may cause you some hardship. If you don't understand why it is undesirable to know your future, think of this: how would you spend your last days if you knew exactly when, where and how you would die? Although you may use your time to some advantage, you would likely spend the rest of your days reacting to that knowledge. Chances are, it would consume your entire energy in either trying to do everything you could before that awesome moment or everything you could to avoid it. Your life would become an unendurable period of second-guessing your future.

If after 15 minutes or so of trying you have had little success, give up for the day. Try again the next day and as many days after as you care to. At the same time, you must improve your knowledge of your technique. You must study. Read all the material you can on the subject, of which there is much. Your local library will provide you with all the standard metaphysical texts, including those in the bibliography of this book. If you achieve some degree of success, you may wish to pursue the interest in earnest. Be careful that it does not become an obsession: you may do yourself a lot of damage that way. Like any new field of endeavor, it is at first so captivating that you are inclined to experience all you can, like a poor boy given all the chocolate cake he can eat. If you find that you are ignoring your spouse or upsetting your family life, take a breather. A few months rest from automatic writing and all things mystical will not harm your learning position. It will only defer it and perhaps even make it more useful to you. Like the summer recess from school, a few months or even years may give your mind a badly needed rest.

Although, as I intimated, there are harmful souls out there, they cannot harm you except through yourself. But make no mistake about it: that is a great danger. The power of automatic writing is its ability to overwhelm your senses and your wisdom. You can be quite easily convinced to do the outrageous, while at the same time fully aware of what you are doing. You will also feel as though it is perfectly natural and acceptable, and may in fact be. Yet society does

Appendix

frown upon many activities it considers abnormal and a social frown is sometimes called ostracization. In other words, if you start acting weird, you may put some distance between yourself and those you love. Again, moderation is the key. If you practice your new interest behind closed doors and don't make it the topic of your every conversation, you shouldn't upset too many friends. But like a new baby, the truths learned through automatic writing instill a great desire in people to show them off. Whatever you do, do not spend more than an hour a day at the task. More than that and the mind tires: tired minds are not the most receptive to learning.

Whatever the outcome of your quest, don't despair. If you are interested in metaphysics and seek to learn of the soul, the information you can gain through automatic writing has already been gained by others and has been published in many forms. So if you fail to achieve the experience, the information (or most of it) is available to be read. And if you grow tired of the technique, its teachings beginning to seem redundant or overly familiar, you may wish to explore other techniques or interests. As your awareness expands, so will your interests. That, after all, is evolution.

GLOSSARY

Accepted Reality An individual's or society's preconception of physical reality, i.e., what is considered within the realm of the possible.

Astral That which relates to immediately higher planes than this atomical plane where the energy matter comprising those planes is called "astral" by souls.

Astral Body That portion of the human being which can traverse from the flesh to higher planes and then return to the flesh; this portion of the physical consciousness is the Spirit.

Astral Projection The projection of the astral body, or Spirit, out of the corporeal body. This removal of a particular level of consciousness is practiced by many people at a specific point between waking and sleeping. Others, more rarely, can astral project while fully awake.

Aura The visible spectrum of light produced by the life-energy of the human body. Although it visibly surrounds the flesh, in actual fact, the energy matter pervades the body and is related to the joining of higher forms of energy with atomically based energies of the corporeal body. All atomical matter has a related aura, though not always multi-colored or as complex as that of living entities.

Base Soul The fundamental part of the life-force; when in flesh, the base soul is the basis of life itself, where instinct and all innate knowledge reside. It provides the primary mechanisms of consciousness which enable the corporeal body to exist as a coherent entity. Out of flesh, the base soul rapidly assimilates the energy of the Spirit, which, in essence, is the byproduct of a soul joining a corporeal body.

Biological Stasis The various identifiable points at which a species (or individuals conforming to special evolution) achieve a plateau of a given type of experience, e.g., the achievement of cognitive reason by man and certain lower orders. There are many forms of biological stasis, each relating to specific characteristics.

Consolidation Any melding together of divergent forces to a unified force. Post-life consolidation is a specific form of consolidation of energy and experience following an incarnation in flesh during which the Base Soul assimilates the Spirit.

Godly Ideals A system of ideals held by superior beings known among souls as the Guides of Man, and, among in-flesh humans, often known as gods or messengers of God.

Guide Anyone who guides, e.g., parents, teachers, souls of loved ones. The Guides of Man are higher order souls who have chosen to involve themselves in guiding the development of human civilization.

Incarnation A lifetime in the flesh. The incarnation ends during the post-life consolidation of the life-experiences and

Glossary

energy matter of the Spirit into the base soul.

Karma The forces of action and reaction as they relate to life. Karma may be good, bad or indifferent but each individual is responsible for ensuring that he causes as little harm to others as possible. Progress in the evolution of the soul occurs when the individual causes more good to result from his actions than harm.

Karmic Courtesy The etiquette of the Soul. Each level of soul has its own intricate patterns of social courtesy, even as social groups of in-flesh humans do. Courtesy is a primary agent in harmonious interaction between individuals.

Karmic Law The principles of evolution within a planet as they relate to the lifeforms of that planet. Although subject to Universal Laws of Nature, Karmic Law is the result of forces peculiar to a given planet and its position in the Cosmos.

Karmic Place The niche in which an individual fits most comfortably or is most suited. This place is determined by reaction to action: prior actions of the individual force inevitable reactions; current actions are efforts to redirect subsequent reactions.

Karmic Way The Way of life chosen by individuals and societies in a relative sense. Every culture is such a Way; however, when souls refer to The Way, they mean the Way of all life, i.e., all the basic influences common to evolving lifeforms. This commonality between lifeforms has a definible progression particularly relevant to the soul.

Life-Energy Any of the essential energies that constitute life. However, in specific reference to the human being, life-energy is the energy of the Spirit, manufactured by the cohesion of a soul to a corporeal body. This life-energy is converted to soul-energy in the post-life consolidation period.

Lower Conscious The consciousness of the base soul, which is not easily accessed by the human mind. It is also called the Base Conscious as it is the base of consciousness for the individual.

Middle Conscious More of a barrier to consciousness than an actual physical construction. It results from the opposing energy forces of the lower conscious and upper conscious and provides much of the machinery for imagination and dream production. In other words, the consciousness of the lower self mixes with the consciousness of the upper self, resulting in mixed up images. When under control, the Middle Conscious is a wonderful tool; when out of control, it can be a maniacal device.

Mind-Energy A specific construction of energies which comprise the human mind. It is integrally a part of the Spirit, or life-energy structure, but does not constitute the entire Spirit. The surface conscious of waking life and its immediate "subconscious", as Freudians might say, are largely the machinations of mind-energy but are also (at times overwhelmingly) influenced by all other levels of consciousness.

Near-Life Amorphous compounds of energy matter which closely resemble those of living forms, but which have yet to achieve even the slightest degree of self-direction, the first stage of life.

Physical Stasis The physical state of matter which holds

Glossary

a given form or structure for a lengthy period of time, e.g., an atom has a physical form of stasis until changed in some fundamental way, as in fission or fusion.

Realm of Effect An entity's immediate sphere of influence, e.g., the immediate social influence of a human being on family, friends and environment.

Reincarnation The cyclical joining of the soul to one corporeal body after another in a predetermined manner. In the evolution of the human soul, reincarnation occurs within the context of one species; souls at other levels of experience may use more than one species, providing the species are closely related. Through reincarnation, souls evolve from lower levels to higher levels of being.

Spirit The principle energy structure of a given incarnation, produced by a base soul joining a corporeal body. The soul, although a form of life-energy itself, is actually the consolidated remains of many prior incarnations and will eventually incorporate the energy and experiences of the Spirit at the end of the incarnation. In this manner, the soul continually grows ("evolves"), each incarnation providing fresh learning experiences. The Spirit, therefore, is a semi-independent energy structure during in-flesh life but is incorporated into the base soul beginning with the death of the corporeal flesh.

Spirit Travel An occult term for astral projection, which may in fact be more accurate. Portions of the Spirit's consciousness are actually transmitted outside the body to gather experience. Although every human being has this *capability,* not all have developed the *ability.*

Soul The Soul, spelled with a capital, is the entire life-force of an entity, particularly entities which have similar properties to animal lifeforms. When in flesh, the Soul exists in two fundamental energy structures: the base soul and the Spirit. Out of flesh, these two energy structures consolidate, to form the Soul.

Soul-Energy That type of energy which comprises the soul. It is formed through the consolidation of less stable life-energy, which is produced during in-flesh life. Soul-energy, once formed, is virtually permanent.

Soul-Memories Soul-energy retains images of past lives just as life-energy retains images of experiences of the current incarnation. Although sometimes very traumatic for the individual, techniques of past-life recall enable the mind (based in life-energy) to call up images from prior lives. These techniques involve passing images through the middle conscious, which normally acts as a screen between the base soul and the mind.

Stasis A temporary resting point or plateau of experience. At such a point, evolution is seemingly arrested, although change in fact simply slows to the miniscule for a period of time. At this point, a relatively small effort or expenditure of energy can cause quite dramatic changes. A ball thrown straight up eventually experiences a form of stasis when it halts at the peak of its flight. At that point, gravity changes its direction but another force, perhaps a tennis racket, could cause an equally dramatic change.

Supreme Stasis Even the universe itself must eventually reach a point of stasis. At this point, I suspect, the universe would achieve a complete uniformity that is so inherently unstable as to produce an immediate explosion, or "Big Bang". I suspect also that the universe has experienced such

Glossary

a stasis many times, perhaps an infinity of times, and will experience many more to infinity. Time, in such a reference, is meaningless.

Universal Laws These are the Laws of Nature, absolutes which cannot be governed, but which do the governing. They determine the nature of reality by being the backbone of reality; as human intelligences, we can only define the properties and mathematical relationships which describe them.

Upper Conscious The human mind. It is the greatest tool of the in-flesh human experience as it guides the body during waking activities. During sleep, however, it takes a back seat to other forces of consciousness, such as the influence of the middle conscious and the base soul.

Way The Way is the absolute principles of social harmony and the evolution of intelligent life. Not all lifeforms have a sufficient grasp of these principles to exercise them as effectively as others; Man, as an animal species, is a long evolutionary step from achieving a truly harmonious Way. Even so, the species is evolving in a predictable manner.

BIBLIOGRAPHY

The books listed below expand the discussion of many areas of my work and have also provided me with valuable background material and understanding. None are offered on any other credentials than those presented by their respective authors.

Adventures in Immortality, by George Gallup, Jr., McGraw-Hill Book Company, Inc., New York, N.Y., 1982. Discusses the results of a series of surveys of U.S. public opinion concerning life after death, particularly in regard to the near-death experience. Very weak in terms of statistical analysis.

Arthur Ford Speaks From Beyond, by Eileen Sullivan, Fawcett Publications, Inc., Greenwich, Connecticut, 1975. Eileen Sullivan records the thoughts of the deceased psychic Arthur Ford through automatic writing. Even if it isn't Ford on the other side, the material represented in this book is consistent with my experiences of automatic writing.

A Search for the Truth, by Ruth Montgomery, William Morrow & Company, Inc., New York, N.Y., 1966. Montgomery's first-person account of her introduction to automatic writing. Her experiences very closely paralleled my own in many ways, including her description of journalistic skepticism.

From Ritual to Romance, by Jessie L. Weston, Doubleday Anchor Books, Doubleday & Company, Inc., Garden City, N.Y., 1957. (Originally published by Cambridge University Press, 1920.) Analyzes the influences of pre-Christian nature rituals in the development of the legend of the Holy Grail.

Hidden Channels of the Mind, by Louisa E. Rhine, William Sloane Assoc., New York, N.Y., 1961. Discusses Extrasensory Perception (ESP) research at Duke University, Durham, North Carolina. Required reading for those who have not yet realized the validity of the ESP experience.

Life After Life, by Dr. Raymond Moody, Jr., Mockingbird Books, Covington, Georgia, 1975. Moody constructs a composite of the "near-death" experience. Discusses commonalities between his case studies and material gleaned from the Tibetan Book of the Dead, the Bible, the works of Plato, etc.

Life at Death: A Scientific Investigation of the Near-Death Experience, by Kenneth Ring, Ph.D, Coward, McCann & Geoghegan, New York, N.Y., 1980. Ring is a psychologist inspired by Moody's book to fill the statistical void left by Moody's and other earlier works. His study definitely supports Moody's findings.

Modern Man in Search of a Soul, by Carl Gustave Jung, Routledge & Kegan Paul Ltd., London, 1933. Describes how the human "unconscious" is reflected in the behavior and attitudes of individual human beings.

Other Worlds: A Portrait of Nature in Rebellion; Space, Superspace and the Quantum Universe, by Paul Davies,

Bibliography

Simon & Schuster, New York, N.Y., 1980. Discusses quantum theories in layman's terms, including a mathematical theory that indicates the plausibility of other planes existing in the same finite space as ours.

Out of the Minds of Babes, by Dr. Otto Weininger, Charles Thomas, Inc., Springfield, Illinois, 1982. A professor of Clinical Child Psychology, Weininger describes the developmental characteristics of children.

Past Lives Therapy, by Morris Netherton, Ph.D., and Nancy Shiffrin, William Morrow & Company, Inc., New York, N.Y., 1978. Netherton describes his technique of using past lives recall to help psychiatric patients overcome problems arising from past life trauma. I have used a similar technique to recall my past lives.

Pheneas Speaks, by Arthur Conan Doyle, The Psychic Press and Bookshop, London, 1926. Doyle transcribes messages from his guide, Pheneas, and others. He also describes various psychic experiences and the techniques he and his family used for contacting the other side.

Psychic Discoveries Behind the Iron Curtain, edited by Sheila Ostrander and Lynn Schroeder, Prentice Hall, Eaglewood Cliffs, N.J., 1970. Includes discussions on many psychic phenomena, including a claim that the human aura has been photographed.

Reincarnation and Science, by Ruth Reyna, Sterling Publishers, New Delhi, 1973. Draws a hypothesis of the "omion", an energy-based counterpart of the meson (a subatomic particle which, theoretically, binds together the atom) as being a primary constituent of soul-energy. My guides suggest that although the omion is the wrong particle, the hypothesis is similar to the facts.

The Evidence for Life After Death, by Martin Ebon, New American Library, New York, N.Y., 1977. Light reading which summarizes the work of various researchers of life after death, including Dr. Moody's.

The Hidden Spectre, compiled by Robert Tralins, Avon Books, New York, N.Y., 1970. Simple case histories of phenomena which do not fit into current scientific paradigms of reality. Tralins provides a list of contacts for those skeptical enough to do some checking.

The Human Aura and How I Teach My Students to See It, by Bevy (Beverly C. Jaegers), The Lumen Press, St. Louis, Missouri, 1971. A concise handbook to introduce you to seeing the auras of humans, plants, animals and even non-living objects.

Theory of Knowledge, Edited by Julius R. Weinberg and Keith E. Yandell, Holt, Rinehart & Winston, Inc., 1971. Draws on historical philosophical arguments to introduce the student to the traditions of Western philosophy.

There is a River: The Story of Edgar Cayce, by Thomas Sugrue, Dell Publishing Co., Inc., New York, N.Y., 1970. (Originally published by Holt, Rinehart & Winston Inc., 1942.) Cayce's story is remarkable but consistent with the experiences of others. The book has a few disturbing flaws as a biography which are probably the result of revisions of the original text.

The Two Hands of God, by Alan W. Watts, George Braziller, Inc., New York, N.Y., 1963. A work of comparative mythology, which shows that the world's

Bibliography

religious myths have many startling similarities.

Understanding Media: The Extensions of Man, by Marshall McLuhan, McGraw-Hill Book Company, Inc., New York, N.Y., 1964. Analyzes the inventions of man, particularly the communications media, as extensions of the human being.

Wolves of Minong, by Durward L. Allen, Houghton Mifflin Company, Boston, 1979. Describes the social organization of the wolf pack.

In addition to the above books, there exist thousands which have been catalogued in various published bibliographies, including the following:

Bibliography of Parapsychology, compiled by George Zorab, Parapsychology Foundation, New York, N.Y., 1957.

Chicorel Index to Parapsychology and Occult Books, edited by Marietta Chicorel, 1978.

Occult Bibliography: An Annotated List of Books Published in English, 1971 through 1975, by Thomas C. Clarie, Scarecrow Press, Metuchen, N.J., 1978.

Psychic and Religious Phenomena Limited: A Bibliographic Index, compiled by Clyde S. King, Westport, Connecticut, Greenwood Press, 1978.

STAYING IN TOUCH

On the following pages you will find listed, with their current prices, some of the books now available on related subjects. Your book dealer stocks most of these, and will stock new titles in the Llewellyn Series as they become available.

However, to obtain our full catalog, and to keep informed of the new titles as they are released, you may write for our bi-monthly newspaper/catalog. A sample copy is free, and it will continue coming to you at no cost as long as you are an active mail customer. Or you may keep it coming for a full year with a donation of just $5.00 ($7.00 for Canada & Mexico, $10.00 overseas, first class mail).

Stay in touch! Included are news and reviews of new books, announcements of meetings and seminars all over the country, articles helpful to our readers, news of our authors, advertising of products and services, etc.

The Llewellyn New Times
P.O. BOX 64383-MUQ, St. Paul, MN 55164-0383, U.S.A.

TO ORDER BOOKS

If your book dealer does not have the books described on the following pages readily available, you may order them direct from the publisher by sending full price in U.S. currency, plus $1.25 each for postage and handling within the United States, $2.00 each for surface mail outside the United States, or $7.00 each for foreign Airmail.

FOR GROUP STUDY AND PURCHASE

Because there is a great deal of interest in Group Discussion and Study of the subject matter of this book, we feel that we should encourage the adoption and use of this particular book by such groups by offering a special "quantity" price to Group Leaders or "Agents".

Our Special Quantity Discount, for a minimum order of five copies of MAN'S UNENDING QUEST, is $29.85, Cash With Order. This price includes postage and handling within the United States. If Minnesota resident, then add the state sales tax. For additional quantities, please order in multiples of five. For Canadian and foreign orders, please inquire. Credit Card (VISA, MasterCard, American Express, Diners' Club) Orders are accepted. Charge Card orders only may be phoned free by dialing 1-800-THE MOON. Mail orders to:

LLEWELLYN PUBLICATIONS
213 E. 4th St., P.O. Box 64383-MUQ
St. Paul, MN 55164-0383, U.S.A.

THE LLEWELLYN PRACTICAL GUIDES
by Melita Denning & Osborne Phillips

THE LLEWELLYN PRACTICAL GUIDE TO ASTRAL PROJECTION.
Yes, your consciousness can be sent forth, out-of-the-body, with full awareness and return with full memory. You can travel through time and space, converse with non-physical entities, obtain knowledge by non-material means, and experience higher dimensions.

> **Is there life-after-death? Are we forever shackled by Time & Space? The ability to go forth by means of the Astral Body, or Body of Light, gives the personal assurance of consciousness (and life) beyond the limitations of the physical body. No other answer to these ageless questions is as meaningful as experienced reality.**

The reader is led through the essential stages for the inner growth and development that will culminate in fully conscious projection and return. Not only are the requisite practices set forth in step-by-step procedures, augmented with photographs and "puts-you-in-the-picture" visualization aids, but the vital reasons for undertaking them are clearly explained. Beyond this, the great benefits from the various practices themselves are demonstrated in renewed physical and emotional health, mental discipline, spiritual attainment, and the development of "extra faculties".

Guidance is also given to the Astral World itself: what to expect, what can be done—including the ecstatic experience of Astral Sex between two people who project together into this higher world where true union is consumated free of the barriers of physical bodies.

0-87542-181-4, 239 pages, 5¼ x 8, softcover $7.95

SUPPLEMENTAL DEEP MIND TAPE
THE LLEWELLYN DEEP MIND TAPE FOR ASTRAL PROJECTION. This is a tool so powerful that it is offered only for use in conjunction with the above book. The authors of this book are adepts fully experienced in all levels of psychic development and training, and have designed this 90-minute cassette tape to guide the student through full relaxation and all the preparations for projection, and then—with the added dimension of the authors personally produced electronic synthesizer patterns of sound and music—they program the Deep Mind through the stages of awakening, and projection of, the astral Body of Light. And then the programming guides your safe return to normal consciousness with memory—enabling you to bridge the worlds of Body, Mind and Spirit.

> **The Deep Mind Tape is a powerful new technique combining guided Mind Programming with specially created sound and music to evoke deep level response in the psyche and its psychic centres for controlled development, and induction of the OUT-OF-BODY EXPERIENCE.**

3-87542-201, 90-minute cassette tape. $9.95
Note: You can order both Book AND Tape for a special price of just $15.00 Postpaid in U.S.A. ($25.00 overseas airmail).

ETERNAL DANCE by LaVedi Laffery & Bud Hollowell
THERE IS NO LIFE AFTER DEATH—THERE IS NO DEATH!

The Spirit is the essence of each individual and it cannot be destroyed. The body and its worldly identity are like suits of clothes you exchange as your True Self moves through one manifestation to another. Explore the incredible world of reincarnation and the implications of its reality in Lafferty and Hollowell's **ETERNAL DANCE,** an exciting new book from Llewellyn Publications.
0-87542-436-8, 512 pp., illustrated. $9.95

ALSO AVAILABLE
Lafferty and Hollowell have developed a series of tapes which are designed to take you into your past lives and allow you to experience those events which have shaped your present personality and existence:

No. 1 HOW PAST LIVES EFFECT THE PRESENT. How Karma works and what it means in your present.

No. 2 HOW TO USE THE POWERS OF HYPNOSIS. Introduction to the basics of self-hypnosis, essential to Past Life exploration.

No. 3 JOURNEY INTO THE PAST WITH A LOVED ONE. Discover the past links between you and those close to you in the present life.

No. 4 FINDING SOLUTIONS TO PRESENT LIFE PROBLEMS. Present problems begin in past situations. Discover the means for important breakthroughs to solutions.

No. 5 DISCOVER HIDDEN TALENTS, ABILITIES AND KNOWLEDGE. Tap the resources from earlier lives. Tapes 3, 4, and 5 have on side two the very effective **BODY OF LIGHT INDUCTION** exercise, designed to help you find peace and a loving center with yourself.

Each tape is $9.95. A set of all five tapes is available for $39.95. You save over $9.00!

To order any Llewellyn books, send full price plus $1.00 postage & handling for each book ($7.00 each overseas airmail) and 6% sales tax if you are a Minnesota resident, to:
LLEWELLYN PUBLICATIONS,
P.O. Box 64383-MUQ, St. Paul, MN 55164-0383, U.S.A.

VISA, MasterCard, American Express and Diners' Club orders accepted. Charge card orders may phone free: 1-800-THE MOON (843-6666).

THE LLEWELLYN PRACTICAL GUIDE TO THE DEVELOPMENT OF PSYCHIC POWERS. You may not realize it, but . . . you already have the ability to use ESP, Astral Vision and Clairvoyance, Divination, Dowsing, Prophecy, Communications with Spirits, Mental Telepathy, etc. WE ALL HAVE THESE POWERS! It's simply a matter of knowing what to do, and then to exercise (as with any talent) and develop them.

Written by two of the most knowledgeable experts in the world of Magick today, this book is a complete course—teaching you, step-by-step, how to develop these powers that actually have been yours since birth. Using the techniques they teach, you will soon be able to move objects at a distance, see into the future, know the thoughts and feelings of another person, find lost objects, locate water and even people using your own no-longer latent talents.

Psychic powers are as much a natural ability as any other talent. You'll learn to play with those new skills, work with groups of friends to accomplish things you never would have believed possible before reading this book. The text shows you how to make the equipment you can use, the exercises you can do—many of them at any time, anywhere—and how to use your abilities to change your life and the lives of those close to you. Many of the exercises are presented in forms that can be adapted as games for pleasure and fun, as well as development. Illustrated throughout.
0-87542-191-1, 244 pages, 5¼ x 8, soft cover. $6.95

THE LLEWELLYN PRACTICAL GUIDE TO PSYCHIC SELF-DEFENSE AND WELL-BEING. Psychic Well-Being and Psychic Self-Defense are two sides of the same coin—just as physical health and resistance to disease are:

    FACT: Each person (and every living thing) is surrounded bide the means to Psychic Self-Defense and to dynamic Well-Being.

This book explores the world of very real "psychic warfare" that we all are victims of:

    FACT: Every person in our modern world is subjected, constantly, to psychic stress and psychological bombardment: advertising and sales promotions that play upon primitive emotions, political and religious appeals that work on feelings of insecurity and guilt, noise, threats of violence and war, news of crime and disaster, etc.

This book shows the nature of genuine psychic attacks—ranging from actual acts of black magic to bitter jealousy and hate—and the reality of psychic stress, the structure of the psyche and its inter-relationship with the physical body. It shows how each person must develop his weakened aura into a powerful defense-shield— thereby gaining both physical protection and energetic well-being that can extend to protection from physical violence, accidents . . . even ill-health.

    FACT: This book can change your life! Your developed aura brings you strength, confidence, poise . . . the dynamics for success, and for communion with your Spiritual Source.

This book gives exact instructions for the fortification of the aura, specific techniques for protection, and the Rite of the First Kathisma using the PSALMS to invoke Divine Blessing. Illustrated with "puts-you-into-the-picture" drawings, and includes powerful techniques not only for your personal use but for group use.
0-87542-190-3, 277 pages, 5¼ x 8, softcover. $7.95